Games for Individualizing
Mathematics Learning

Games for Individualizing Mathematics Learning

LEONARD M. KENNEDY

California State University
Sacramento

RUTH L. MICHON

San Juan Unified School District
Sacramento

Charles E. Merrill Publishing Company
A Bell & Howell Company
Columbus, Ohio

Published by
Charles E. Merrill Publishing Company
A Bell & Howell Company
Columbus, Ohio

International Standard Book Number: 0-675-08937-9

Library of Congress Catalog Card Number: 73-75681

2 3 4 5 6 7 8 9 10–77 76 74 74 73

Printed in the United States of America

Preface

Research into learning indicates that children's concepts and skills develop gradually following a series of definite stages. In mathematics, children need time and materials to work through the stages from concrete to abstract. Carefully selected games can be used to give them opportunities to develop their understandings of concepts and to master skills.

Two recent developments help teachers fit games and other learning activities to the needs of children. (1) Performance objectives provide a means for organizing the curriculum. Once broad goals are established, performance objectives state in explicit ways what children will do to demonstrate progress toward each goal. (2) Teachers are receiving more assistance in their classrooms. Aides, both paid and volunteer, help many teachers prepare materials and work with children.

This book is designed for teachers who want to use games as one way to individualize learning in mathematics. Performance objectives are given for six areas of mathematics: (1) Meaning of Numbers, (2) Operations on Numbers, (3) Measurement, (4) Geometry, (5) Probability and Statistics, and (6) Logic. Each objective is followed by one or more games that will help accomplish it. The games can be made by a teacher or aide using readily available, inexpensive materials. The games can be used by children alone or under the direction of their teacher or an aide. They are for children at levels normally associated with mathematics in the kindergarten through grade six.

The introduction discusses how to use games as a means of individualizing children's learning of mathematics. It contains suggestions for making games, organizing the classroom to use them, and storing and retrieving them.

The authors gratefully acknowledge the help of Joy Jackson, Joanne Click, and Carolann Parsons for their assistance with materials and the manuscript for this book. They also express thanks to the many teachers with whom they have worked for ideas and suggestions about games.

Contents

INTRODUCTION

This book for preservice and inservice teachers contains games for elementary school children. It also contains performance objectives for mathematics which can be used to organize the curriculum so that children's efforts are directed toward learning significant concepts and skills in a meaningful way. Objectives for each child are based on his understanding of mathematics as determined by diagnostic tests and other procedures. Once objectives are selected, a teacher must help a child choose appropriate ways to accomplish them. One way is through games.

Rarely will all children in a classroom be working on the same objective simultaneously. Therefore, there should be many games so that children in pairs or small groups can select and play one designed to help them meet an immediate objective. The games in this book are for small numbers of children—often only two, usually three to five or six.

In this text, the teacher is given a performance objective, then one or more games associated with it. Instructions for preparing materials are given along with frequent illustrations. There are card, board, dice, domino, bingo and lotto games, as well as some of miscellaneous types. Teachers are encouraged to make these games and use them as models for creating their own to cover other concepts and skills. The names of commercial games are listed at the ends of most sections, and the names and addresses of distributors are listed in the appendix.

WHY USE MATHEMATICAL GAMES?

Those associated with children in the classroom know that many problems arise when helping children learn mathematics. These problems result from many causes.

The uncertainty connected with how children learn mathematics is one cause of problems. Research and past experience do not give us prescriptions to follow. Instead, we have only generalizations about how children learn. We know, for example, that a child's understanding of a concept does not emerge full-blown after one or two exposures but develops in stages over a period of time. A child's understanding begins as he manipulates concrete materials, grows as he works with representations of objects and ideas, and matures when he grasps the abstract concepts that come from earlier work. Attempts to shortcut the process by having children work at an abstract level without benefit of earlier concrete and representational work are almost certainly doomed to failure.

We know, too, that a child should actively participate in the learning process at all stages. He must manipulate objects, not merely watch others do it. He must learn to question, reason, and discover patterns as he refines his understanding of concepts and processes. Then he must form his own generalizations about the ideas with which he has been dealing.

Moreover, children's rates of learning vary. A concept or skill that comes easily and quickly to one child is difficult for another. Repeated exposures in many settings are required for the child who learns slowly. Not only do children vary in their learning rates but also in the background they bring to school. A child who has a rich and diverse background is generally ready for more advanced work in mathematics than one whose background is meager.

Games help teachers overcome problems connected with how children learn mathematics. They give children variety in the way they deal with a topic, allow them to actively participate in the learning process, provide repeated exposures without becoming tiresome, and enrich children's backgrounds.

The shift from teacher-centered classrooms characterized by traditional instructional techniques to child-centered classrooms characterized by newer teaching techniques that involve children in individualized learning situations results in problems. There are problems connected with matching children with appropriate materials and activities. A teacher needs a wide variety of materials to make effective matches so that children learn to work efficiently and effectively. Once children learn to work independently, a teacher can make economical use of his time to work with children who need his attention, plan activities, and do the many other things required of him. Games help lessen the problems connected with making the shift from a traditional to modern means of teaching. They give children a readily available source of meaningful activities.

The requirement that children have opportunities to maintain the skills and concepts they learn results in problems. Teachers have traditionally used textbooks and flash cards to give children practice. While these are used successfully by some children, other children quickly tire of the same materials day after day. Children who are bored are not likely to benefit from practice, so teachers must guard against children reaching this state of mind.

Games can be used with other materials to liven practice sessions and heighten children's interest in maintaining skills and concepts. Children are excited by the approach to learning offered by games that bring them face to face with mathematics they might otherwise avoid. And those who win the games—and all children should compete in groups wherein each one wins from time to time—receive immediate reward for their efforts. The sense of accomplishment experienced through winning often encourages a child to try still other mathematical activities.

In addition to these values, games contribute to a successful mathematics program in other ways. Children learn to follow directions, be observant, and develop restraint as they play. They also learn to cooperate, even when competing against others and to accept responsibility for personal as well as group actions.

HOW TO USE MATHEMATICAL GAMES

Teachers who have used games successfully in the past will find it easy to add games from this book to their collection. Others will find these guideline helpful:

1. *Begin small.* Select a game for a group of children to meet one of their performance objectives. Introduce the game to the group, not the entire class. Emphasize the purpose of the game so children's attention is focused on learning rather than fun. They will be aware that a game is fun without being told. And, if they don't think it's fun, no amount of telling them it is will change their minds. Give them a model to follow by playing the game with them the first time. Make

the rules and standards of play clear so children will not interrupt your work with others to get questions answered and rules interpreted.

2. *Increase the number of games and participants.* Select new games for other children and gradually introduce them as needed.

3. *Encourage children to use games frequently.* An informal setting with a table and chairs in a corner invites children to play. Carpeting on the floor reduces noise. Praise children for using games effectively and for learning mathematical facts and skills.

4. *Make games a part of the program.* Children should view a game as an integral part of the mathematics program rather than as a reward for completing an assignment or doing good work.

5. *Evaluate each game's effectiveness.* There are several considerations to make. a) Is it serving the purpose for which it was intended? b) Is it meeting the educational needs of your children? c) Does it present its concepts clearly? d) Does it motivate children to learn the facts or skills associated with it?

6. *Let children make their own games.* Give them a board and playing materials and suggest that they make up ways to play. Provide materials children can use to make original games. Help them select a performance objective to work on and give them materials for cards, a game board, or whatever they may need for their game.

TYPES OF GAMES

Most mathematical games are classified under one of five general types: card, domino, bingo and lotto, board, and dice. Games of each type are included in this book.

Card Games

There are five different types of card games. *Rummy-type games* require that players form sets of cards (books) by taking them from a draw or discard pile. This book includes descriptions of Division Rummy and Fraction Rummy. *Games of Rook* are like Bridge in that all cards are dealt and players take tricks by playing cards of highest value. The game Take a Trick is of this type. In *Old Maid-type games* all cards are dealt and each player draws from an opponent to match and play sets. The player holding the extra card loses. Monster Fractions is based on Old Maid. *Games of Fish* are similar to Old Maid, except that a player asks his opponent for cards of a particular type to match ones he holds. The player making the most matches wins. Place Value Probe and Pick are played this way. Finally, there are *war-type games* where all cards are dealt and turned over simultaneously by players who watch for matching pairs. The player who first claims a match gets all turned-up cards. War-type games in this book are Fract Match and Big G Geometry Match.

Domino Games

There are two types of domino games. Some are played with regular playing pieces. Special rules adapt the game so it can be used for teaching mathematics. Multiplication Domino has rules that make the game useful for helping children understand multiples of numbers. Sets of domino-like playing pieces can be made for games that deal with topics that cannot be covered with regular dominoes. Geometry Dominoes is of this type.

Bingo and Lotto Games

There are many bingo and lotto games that can be devised for mathematics. They are suitable for all topics and children of every age. Wormy Apples Bingo is a game of linear measurement for children just learning about the concept. Gengo and Geometry Lotto deal with geometry.

Board Games

There are no limits to the topics for which board games can be made. These games are both open ended and closed. An open-ended board is one which can be adapted to many topics. The game with the football field used for addition on page 43 also can be used for games dealing with all operations on whole or fractional numbers and other topics as well. Other open-ended boards are Trip to Happy Face, Sports Car Rally, and Horse Race. Closed boards are used for one game only. Simple Simon's Pies, Octacord, Treasure Hunt, and Odd-Even Race are closed board games. Moves on both types of boards are governed by drawing cards, throwing dice, or turning a spinner.

Dice Games

The two probability games included in this book use dice. In one, a single die is used, while in the other a die is used along with colored cubes. These games have a purpose that is different from most others. Children use them to learn about the chances of a particular event or series of events occurring. For example, when children play Odd-Even Race they should keep a record of the number of times each one wins. After many games, players should recognize that the chances are fifty-fifty that either will win.

Miscellaneous Games

There are a variety of games that cannot be put into one of the general categories described above. This book contains concentration, addition and multiplication table, hopscotch, and other miscellaneous games.

HOW TO MAKE GAMES

Classroom games are easy to make, although carefully made games require time. Most materials for games are available to teachers through district supply lists and school supply houses. The list that follows contains all the materials needed for games in this book.

> railroad board—various colors
> three-by-five-inch cards—various colors
> felt pens—broad and fine tipped, various colors
> pencil
> foot ruler and yardstick
> scissors
> glue—white
> rubber cement
> contact paper—clear and colored
> 1/4 inch masonite board
> Magna-hold Paperboard*

---

*Magna-hold Paperboard and Magna Tape are made by Magna-Visual, Inc., and are available from Metro Supply Company, 1420 47th Avenue, Sacramento, California 95822.

Magna Tape*
yarn or string
dice
markers for game boards
library card pockets

There are several ways to equip a room with games. In addition to making them himself, a teacher can often find help. Many teachers have aides, paid or volunteer, who can make games. In addition, game-making sessions with parents can be held. These can be organized by a teacher or a PTA or parent's club. Materials, directions, and sample games are assembled so parents can spend an afternoon or evening making games. High school art teachers are also a source of help, as they can supply names of art students who are willing to make games.

The instructions and illustrations give guidance for making each game. With an opaque projector, patterns for board games can be projected and traced onto a sheet of railroad board. The models at the back of the book can be put on tracing paper and transferred to railroad board or other material to be cut and assembled. The appearance and durability of a board or set of cards are improved if they are covered with clear contact paper. To complete a board, mount it on a piece of masonite with glue or rubber cement. Cut the contact paper so there are about two inches extra at each edge. Roll the paper and peel back four inches of the protective backing. Put two inches of the paper on the back of the masonite. Then fold the paper over the board's edge and press it onto the playing surface. Slowly unpeel the protective backing as you unroll the paper and press it into place. Fold the remaining paper over the board's edge and press it down. Go over the entire surface with a barely warm iron to press out any bubbles and make the contact paper adhere to the railroad board.

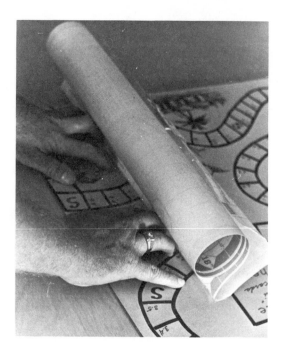

Playing cards are permanently protected from dirt and peeling when they are covered with clear contact paper on both sides. Put a piece of paper smooth side down on a flat surface and unpeel the protective backing. Put the cards on the paper leaving one-half inch between each one. Remove the backing from another piece of paper and put it sticky side down on top of the card-covered first piece. Press the two papers to the cards and each other. Separate the cards by cutting mid-way between each pair. Leave the quarter inch of contact paper around each card to keep it from coming apart.

HOW TO STORE GAMES

Most school rooms are equipped with shelves and closets that can be used to store games. Even so, special storage containers help organize materials. Pencil and hosiery boxes covered with colored contact paper are good for keeping playing pieces together. Corrugated boxes are inexpensive and will hold collections of games. Label each box so children can get and return games quickly.

Specially made storage racks provide space for boards and the boxes that contain their playing pieces, cards, and directions. The rack in the photo on page 10 holds up to forty-eight boards. The upright bins hold four boards apiece, while the ones between them hold the boxes of playing pieces. The upright and large horizontal bins on top are open through the rack so boards can be taken from either side. The box bins are open on one side only, with a set on each side of the rack.

COUNTING

Given a set containing no more than six objects, the student will name the cardinal number of the set.

ROLL EM AND COUNT EM
(2–4 Players)

Preparation

This game requires a die, some objects for players to count, and some tokens to award children for correct answers. Cards containing pictures of sets one to six may be used in place of objects.

Directions

1. Put the objects in the playing area within reach of each player.
2. The first player rolls the die and selects enough objects to make a set of the size indicated by the dots. If he is correct he earns a token.
3. The second player rolls the die and counts enough objects to match.
4. Play continues until all players have had an equal number of turns.
5. The winner is the player with the most tokens.

Variations: 1. Use two dice and have children count more objects.
2. Have numeral cards for a player to match with his set after he has made it.

Given a number line from 0 to 25, the student will count a
number of steps from one number to another.

NUMBER-LINE WALK OFF
(*3–5 Players*)

Preparation

Make a number line (0–25) on the floor with masking tape. Twelve
inches between points is a good distance. Make a set of twenty-five
numeral cards on four-inch squares of railroad board. Lay them along
the line to identify the points. On three-by-five-inch cards, make three
sets of domino cards each containing one, two, three, . . . nine dots.

Directions

1. Choose one child to be the game's leader. He shuffles the domino
   cards and holds them so that they are hidden from the players.
2. The players form a line to the left of the number line with the first
   one standing on zero. The leader gives the first player a domino
   card. The player counts the dots, tells how many there are, and
   takes that many steps along the line. He stands on the point where
   he stops.
3. The leader gives the second player a card. He completes his turn.
4. After each player has had a turn the leader gives the first player a
   second card. The player counts the dots, tells how many there are,
   and takes that many more steps along the line.
5. Play continues until one player reaches or passes 25. The winner is
   the one who reaches 25 first.

Variations: 1. Use numeral cards (1–9) instead of domino cards.
              2. Have children begin at 25 and walk to 0.

Given the numerals 1 through 9, the student will demonstrate that he understands the quantity each one represents
by counting objects.

TRIP TO HAPPY FACE
(*2–4 Players*)

Preparation

Make a Happy Face playing board on a twenty-two-by-twenty-eight-inch piece of railroad board. Cut eighteen two-by-three-inch numeral cards. Draw happy faces on nine of these and sad faces on the other nine. Mark each of the numerals 1 through 9 on the cards in each set. A marker for each child and a die are also needed.

TRIP TO HAPPY FACE

Trip to
Happy Face
Starts Here

FIGURE 1

Directions

1. Shuffle the two sets of cards and put them in their boxes on the playing board. Each player puts his marker on the starting box.
2. The players roll the die to see who goes first. The player with the smallest number of dots goes first.
3. The first player rolls the die and counts the dots. He moves his marker along the board that many spaces. When he stops on a face he takes either a smiling face or a sad face, depending upon which type of face he stopped on. Numerals on smiling faces tell how far a player can advance his marker. Numerals on sad faces tell how far he must move his marker backward.
4. Play continues with players taking their turns in order.
5. The winner is the first child to reach the big happy face.

DELIVER THE MILK
(2 Players)

Preparation

Make an eight-apartment house from a twenty-two-by-twenty-eight-inch piece of railroad board. Glue a strip of magna-hold paperboard on the floor of each apartment. Number the apartments. Cut forty-four small milk bottles from railroad board. Put a piece of magna tape on the back of each bottle. Mark a set of eight three-by-five-inch cards with numerals, one for each apartment. Have some colorful tokens to award children for correct answers.

Directions

1. Put the apartment house on a bulletin board or in a chalk rail. Put the numeral cards face down near the house and the milk bottles where each player can reach them.
2. The first player turns over the top numeral card. He tells its number and puts milk bottles to match in the corresponding apartment. For example, if he turns over numeral card 5, he counts five bottles and puts them on apartment number 5. If he is correct he earns a token. If not, he returns the card and bottles and waits for his next turn.
3. The second player takes a card, reads it, and puts milk bottles in the correct apartment.

FIGURE 2

4. Play continues until all the milk has been delivered.
5. The winner is the player with the most tokens.

DRAW SQUARES
(3–4 Players)

Preparation

Mark one hundred 1 1/2-inch squares on a railroad board. Separate them into sets of ten and mark the squares of each set with one of the shapes illustrated in Figure 3, using a different shape for each set. Cut the squares apart. Next, make a playing board for each child. A board contains a picture of each square along the left edge, space for squares themselves, and lines on which the total number of each type of square is written. Cover each board with clear contact paper to

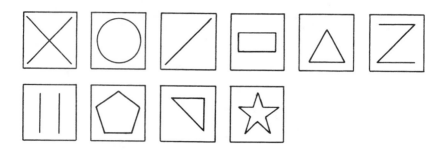

FIGURE 3

make it reusable. Have children write on it with a grease pencil. Use sixty three-by-five-inch cards for draw cards. Put directions for drawing squares on each card (Figure 5) and include instructions to draw one of each shape, two of each shape, through six of each shape.

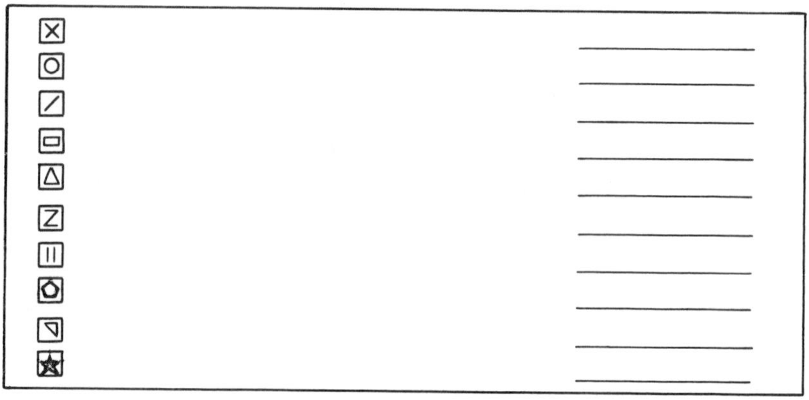

FIGURE 4

Directions

1. Each player has a playing board. Shuffle the direction cards and put them face down. Put the squares face up within reach of each player.

2. The first player takes the top card, turns it face up on the table, and takes as many squares as it directs. He puts the squares in a line behind their kind on the playing board.

FIGURE 5

3. Play continues with each player taking his turn in order.

4. If a player finds there are too few squares of a kind to complete a play according to directions from the card he drew, he loses his turn for that round.

5. Play ends when all squares have been drawn or all direction cards have been played.

6. At the end of play, the players count each type of square they have collected and write the numeral that tells how many are on their boards. When the counting has been completed, the players compare to see who has the most of each type of square. The player with the most squares of one type gets a token. The winner is the player with the most tokens after all squares have been completed.

PLACE VALUE

Given an abacus, the student will use it to represent numbers through 999.

ABACUS ADD ON
(2-6 Players)

Preparation

Each player needs an abacus. If you do not have a commercial abacus for each player, let children make their own. A simple one is made from a styrofoam meat tray, three five-inch pieces of coat hanger wire, Plaster of Paris, and Cheerios. Mix Plaster of Paris and fill the meat tray. Before it sets, stick the wires in to make a three-rod abacus (See Figure 6). The Cheerios are used as abacus beads. The game requires one or two 0–9 spinners. Directions for making a spinner are found on page 147 of the Appendix.

Directions

1. Each player uses an abacus and thirty to forty beads. Use one spinner if the winning score is 100 or less; use two spinners (one for tens and the other for ones) if the score is 250 or more.

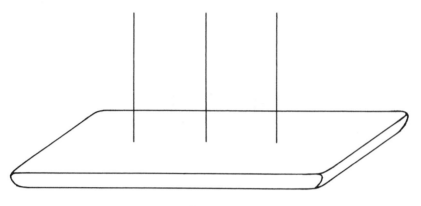

FIGURE 6

2. Each player spins to see who will play first. Use either the high or low number to decide.
3. The first player spins the pointer. When it stops he puts beads on his abacus to show the number he got. (When two spinners are used, one is designated as the ten's spinner, the other as the one's. When the pointers stop, the player reads the ten's spinner and then the one's spinner to get his number.)
4. Each player takes his turn in order to complete the first round.
5. The first player spins again. He puts more beads on his abacus to record the second number. If he goes beyond ten, he exchanges ten beads from the one's wire for one bead on the ten's wire.
6. Play continues until one player reaches the agreed upon total for the round.

PLACE-VALUE MACHINE
(6 Players)

Preparation

Cut three five-by-ten-inch cards from railroad board. Write "Hundreds" on one, "Tens" on another, and "Ones" on the other. Tie a piece of string to each card so it will hang from the back of a chair. Select fifty numbers from 100 to 999 and write their numerals on fifty three-by-five-inch cards, putting one to a card. When completed, each card will look like the one in Figure 7.

FIGURE 7

Directions

1. The six players are divided into two teams of three players each.
2. Hang the signs in order on the backs of the three chairs.
3. The players of one team sit in the chairs with their backs to the members of the other team.
4. A member of the standing team shuffles the cards and puts them

face down. One member of the team picks up the top card and reads the numeral written on it.

5. Each player on the seated team holds up one or both hands with fingers extended to show the number in the place-value position he represents.

6. The players on the standing team check the results by looking at the picture on the numeral card.

7. The seated team scores a point if its response is correct. They stay in the chairs and the other team draws another card. If the response is incorrect the teams exchange places and continue the game.

8. The winning team is the one that scores ten points.

Given numerals for numbers from 10 through 999, the student will represent them using simple expanded notation.

EXPANDED-NOTATION CONCENTRATION
(2 Players)

Preparation

Cut sixteen three-by-four-inch cards from one color of railroad board. Mark eight of them to show tens and eight to show ones, as illustrated in Figure 8. Cut eight three-by-four-inch cards from railroad board of another color. Mark them with compact numerals. A pocket chart is needed.

Directions

1. Hang the pocket chart near a table.
2. Put the compact numeral cards along the right side of the pocket chart, one card to a pocket.
3. Put the expanded numeral cards face down in a four-by-four array.
4. The first player turns over two cards. If the cards show the expanded form of one of the numerals in the pocket chart, he puts them in the pocket to the left of the numeral card and turns over another pair. If the cards do not go together, they are returned to their face-down positions on the table.

2 tens +	3 ones =	23
5 tens +	8 ones =	58
7 tens +	1 one =	71
8 tens +	2 ones =	82
4 tens +	6 ones =	46
6 tens +	0 ones =	60
9 tens +	9 ones =	99
1 ten +	5 ones =	15

FIGURE 8

5. The other player turns over two cards. If he makes an expanded numeral he puts them in the pocket chart. If not, he returns them to the table.
6. Play continues until the sixteen cards have been correctly matched with their compact numerals.
7. The winner is the player who completes more expanded numerals.

(Make several sets of cards, using different numerals, so children will have more than one game. Be sure each set has eight different numbers for tens and eight different numbers for ones.)

PLACE-VALUE PROBE
(3–6 Players)

Preparation

Make twelve sets of three cards each on three-by-five-inch cards. Mark each set so it contains the same number expressed in three ways. Figure 9 shows 234 in its compact form, expanded form, and on the abacus. Select other numerals between 100 and 999 for the remaining eleven sets.

 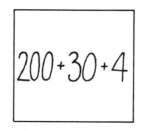 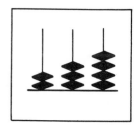

FIGURE 9

Directions

1. The dealer shuffles the cards and deals them all to the players.
2. Players must organize their cards into books, matching the three cards which express the same number. Players who have three cards of a kind put them face up where all players can see them.
3. The first player asks any one of the other players for a card to match one of the pairs or single cards he holds. He must ask for the card by name. For example, "I want you to give me the expanded form of 234." If he gets the card to complete a book he puts the book face up on the table and takes another turn. If he gets a card but does not complete a book he puts the card in his hand and takes another turn. If he does not get a card his turn is over for the round.
4. Play continues with each player taking his turns in order.
5. The game is over when one player is rid of all of his cards.
6. A player scores three points for each book he completes. He loses two points for each pair of cards and one point for each single card he holds.
7. The winner is the player with the most points.

EXPANDO LAND
(2–4 Players)

Preparation

Make an open-ended game board on a piece of twenty-two-by-twenty-eight-inch railroad board. The game board illustrated in Figure 10 has a Disneyland theme. Cut forty-eight two-by-three-inch cards from railroad board. Write "EXPANDO" on twenty-four and put a Mickey

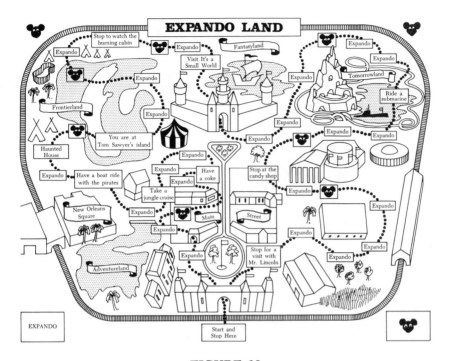

FIGURE 10

Mouse head on the other twenty-four. The Expando cards contain these problems.

What is the expanded notation of 639?
111 = _____ hundreds + _____ tens + _____ ones
What is the expanded notation of 258?
6 tens + 13 ones = _____
62 tens + 4 ones = _____
200 + 6 = _____
907 = _____ tens + _____ ones
There are _____ hundreds in 946
7 hundreds + 5 tens = _____
930 = _____ tens
7 hundreds + 0 tens + 8 ones = _____
300 + 60 + 9 = _____
793 = _____ hundreds + _____ tens + _____ ones
582 = _____ hundreds + _____ tens + _____ ones

FIGURE 11

There are _____ ones in 452
6 hundreds + 4 tens + 7 ones = _____
There are _____ tens in 999
There are _____ hundreds in 272
There are _____ tens in 367
15 tens and 7 ones = _____
What is the expanded notation of 152?
200 + 30 = _____
600 + 90 + 4 = _____
There are _____ tens in 409.

(Use numbers beyond 999 for children who are working with larger numbers.)

The Mickey Mouse cards contain these directions:

You hit the target at the shooting gallery and win an extra turn.
What's all the excitement up ahead? Go ahead 3 spaces to see.
There's a band playing down the street. Go back 4 spaces to hear it.
You say "Hi" to Mickey Mouse and he gives you an extra turn.
   Take it now.
Tom Sawyer invites you to his island. Join him there.

The people of Small World sing to you. Go there to listen.

You turned in a lost purse. Your reward is an extra turn.

The burning cabin is almost gone. Go see if you can save any of it.

The submarine is ready to go down. Hurry—get aboard.

You are thirsty. Go have a coke.

The Haunted House haunts you. Go there to visit ghosts.

The Candy Shop has good chocolate bars. Go get one.

All this walking has made you tired. Stop and rest. Lose a turn.

In New Orleans Square there's a boat ride. Go to it.

When you get hungry and stop to eat you lose a turn.

Go to Adventureland for the Jungle Cruise.

You are lost. Go back 3 spaces to find out where you are.

Mr. Lincoln has a message for you. You are lucky because you are going to hear it.

You slip while climbing the Matterhorn and lose a turn.

You stop to feed the ducks by the dock. Lose a turn.

You help a child find a lost ticket in Fantasyland. Take an extra turn.

You forgot film for your camera. Go back 2 spaces to buy some.

You want come cotton candy. Go ahead 3 spaces to buy some.

Pluto calls you. Go ahead 2 spaces to see what he wants.

Make a key so players can check answers during the game. One die is needed.

Directions

1. Each player puts his marker at the entrance to Expando Land. Shuffle the EXPANDO and MOUSE cards and put them face down in their boxes on the game board.
2. The first player rolls the die and moves his marker the number of spaces it indicates. When a play ends on an EXPANDO space, the player picks up an EXPANDO card and answers its question. If the answer is correct, his marker remains where it is. If it is incorrect, the marker is moved back to its position when the play began. When a play ends on a MICKEY MOUSE space, the player picks up a MOUSE card and follows the directions on it. A player makes no response when his play ends on any of the other spaces.
3. Play continues with each player taking his turns in order.
4. The winner is the player who is first to move his marker around the board and out of EXPANDO LAND.

Given a number from 100 through 999, the student will tell how many hundreds, tens, and ones are in it.

SPIN A VALUE
(3–6 Players)

Preparation

Make a place-value card holder with three pockets for each player. (Directions for making a pocket card holder are on page 150 of the Appendix.) Mark lines to separate the pockets. Label the pockets Hundreds, Tens, and Ones. Cut thirty two-by-four-inch cards from

8	6	1
Hundreds	Tens	Ones

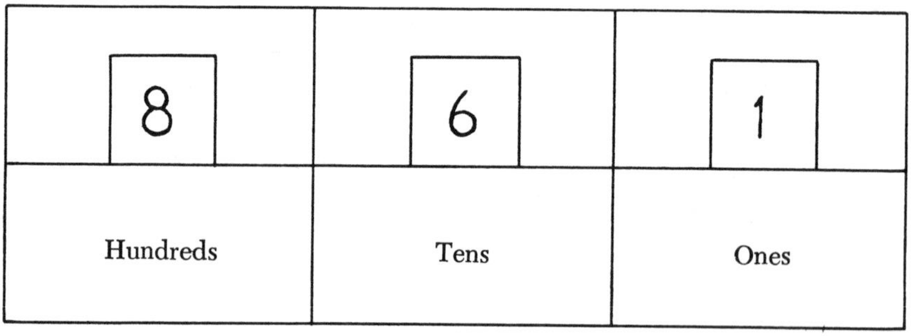

FIGURE 12

another color of railroad board for each player. Make three sets of ten cards each; mark each with the numerals 0 through 9. Cut twelve two-by-four-inch cards from railroad board. Write "Go High" on four, "Go Low" on four, and "Go High or Low" on the remaining four. A spinner is needed. (Directions for making a spinner are on page 147 of the Appendix.)

Directions

1. Each player has a place-value card holder and three sets of numeral cards.
2. Shuffle the twelve direction cards and put them face down. Turn over the top card and place it beside the pile. This card guides the

play for the first round. If it says "Go High" players will try to make the numeral for the largest three-place number possible from three spins. If it says "Go Low" they will try for the smallest three-place number possible from three spins. If it says "Go High or Low" the players will try for either the largest or smallest three-place number.

3. One player spins the spinner. The number it stops on is used for the first play of the round. Each player picks a numeral card for that number and puts it in one of the pockets of his card holder. If the direction card says "Go High" the numeral card is put in the pocket where the player thinks it will help make the numeral for the largest number from three spins. If he is trying for the smallest number the card is put where he thinks it will help make its numeral.

4. A player spins the spinner a second time. Players put the numeral card in one of the two open pockets.

5. A player spins the spinner a third time. Now each player puts the third card in the open pocket of the holder. (Once a player has put a numeral card in the holder he cannot change it from one pocket to another.)

6. At the end of a round each player reads the numeral in his card holder. The winner of a round is the player whose numeral represents the largest or smallest number, according to the direction card for that round. Each player keeps his own score. (There may be several winners each round.)

7. After a round has been completed, turn over a new direction card and play another round.

8. Play continues until twelve rounds have been completed.

9. The winner is the player who scores the most points. A point is scored for each winning or tying number.

Variations: Increase the size of the card holder and number of spins so players can write names for numbers in the thousands and millions.

Commercial games that reinforce understanding of place value:

Abacus Spinner Game
Place Value I
Place Value II
　(Creative Publications)

ADDITION

Given the 100 basic addition combinations, the student will name the sums.

APPLE TREE ADDITION
(2–6 Players)

Preparation

Make a nine-by-twelve-inch game board for each player. A game board contains a picture of an apple tree drawn on a piece of railroad board. Glue twelve circular pieces of magna-hold paperboard to the branches. Mark each piece with one of the basic addition combinations. Put a different set of combinations on each board. Cut a set of twelve red apples from railroad board for each player. Put a small piece of magna tape on the back of each apple. Make a set of cards containing the sums for the 100 basic addition combinations. Have an addition table available so players can check answers at the end of a game.

Directions

1. Each player has a playing board and twelve apples.
2. The leader mixes the sum cards and puts them face down in a box. He draws one and tells the players what it is.

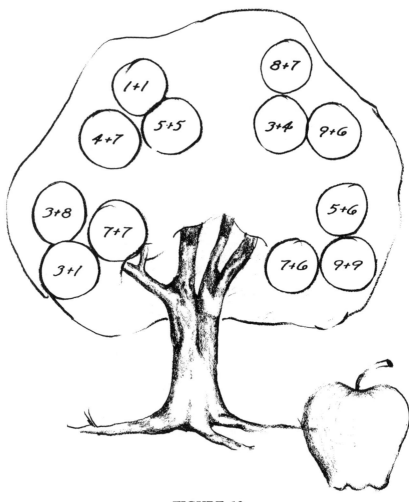

FIGURE 13

3. If a player has a combination that equals the sum, he puts an apple on his tree.
4. Play continues with the leader giving sums and the players putting apples on their trees.
5. The winner is the player to cover his tree with apples first.

Variation: Put subtraction, multiplication, or division combinations on the tree. Make cards containing differences, products, or quotients.

CLOTHESPIN WHEEL
(*2–4 Players*)

Preparation

From railroad board, cut a circle with a six-inch diameter for each player. Mark each wheel as shown in Figure 14. Make a set of ten clothespins for each player. Write "0" on one, "1" on another, and so on to "9" on the last one. Three dice are needed.

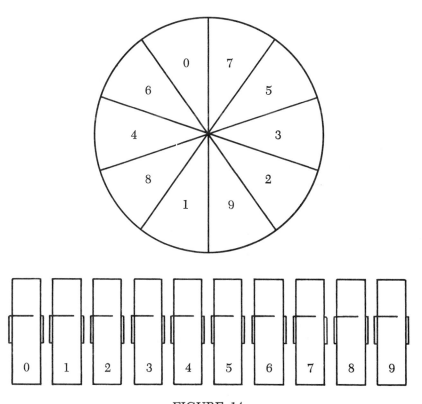

FIGURE 14

Directions

1. Each player has a wheel. Put all the clothespins in a box and mix them. Each player takes a set of ten clothespins from the box without regard to the numerals on them.
2. The leader rolls the dice. He counts the dots and tells how many there are. This number is the sum for the first round.

3. Each player clips one of his clothespins onto his card so the sum of the numerals of the clothespin and the card equal the sum shown on the dice. If a player does not have a clothespin to put on the wheel to make a sum for the round, he waits for the next round.

4. The leader tosses the dice again and counts the dots. This number is the sum for the second round.

5. Each player again clips a clothespin onto his card.

6. The game continues until ten rounds are completed.

7. The winner is the player who has clipped the most clothespins to his card.

ADD A PETAL
(2–4 Players)

Preparation

Make a flower set for each player. A set consists of three two-inch flower centers and twenty-four petals cut from railroad board. Cut the petals so eight will fit around one center. Mark the centers with such sums as 13, 14, and 15. Write addition combinations for these sums on the petals. Put pieces of magna tape on the back of each center and petal. One die is needed. Make a key so players can check answers as the game is played.

Directions

1. Each player puts his flower centers on a magnetic board. He puts his petals face up where he can reach them easily.

2. The first player rolls the die to determine how many of his petals he can put up during the first round. He chooses petals and puts them around one or more of his centers. As he puts each petal in place he tells the combination and its sum, e.g., "12 plus 2 equals 14." If a player puts a wrong combination with a sum, he does not get to add the petal to the flower.

3. Play continues with each player taking his turn in order.

4. The winner is the player who completes his three flowers first. (Make several games using different sums and combinations so children can practice adding different numbers.)

FIGURE 15

RALLY RACE
(*2–5 Players*)

Preparation

Make a game board similar to the one in Figure 16. Cut thirty two-by-three-inch cards from railroad board. Write "Add _____ to each number you pass," filling in the blank with 0 on three cards, 1 on three, through 9 on the last three. Cut another twenty two-by-three-inch cards. Write "Rally" on one side of each card. Put one of the following instructions on the other side of each of the cards.

You ran out of gas and have to get some more. Go back 3 spaces.
You have a flat tire and must wait for a repair truck. Lose 1 turn.

FIGURE 16

Your engine overheats and you need repairs. Lose 1 turn.

You stop to help put out a fire in another car. Take an extra turn to make up for lost time.

The weather has cooled and you are running well. Move ahead 4 spaces.

You get hot and thirsty. Stop for water. Lose 1 turn.

Your new engine is putting out lots of power. Move ahead 3 spaces.

You stop to give directions to a lost driver. Take an extra turn.

You find a secret shortcut. Move ahead 2 spaces.

The rains are making the roadway slippery. Slow down. Lose 1 turn.

You miss a turn in the dark. Go back 3 spaces.

You help a driver get his car back on the road. Take an extra turn.

ɪou stop to put a road sign back up. Take an extra turn.

Your car overheats. Go back 2 spaces for water.

Your map blows out the window. Go back 1 space to pick it up.

You are coasting down a long hill. Move ahead 2 spaces.

Your headlights aren't working. Go back 3 spaces to have them repaired.

You are rested after a pit stop. Move ahead 3 spaces.

The sun dries up the track. You can speed up. Move ahead 2 spaces.

A bridge is washed out. Go back 3 spaces to detour around it.

A pair of dice and a marker for each child are needed.

Directions

1. Each player puts his marker at the starting position for the race. The RALLY and addition cards are put in their places on the board.
2. The first player rolls the dice to determine how far he will move. Then he picks up an addition card. He adds the number from the card to numbers on the board as he moves his marker. If he gives a wrong sum for a pair of numbers, he stops on the space where he gave the last correct answer. When a move ends on a RALLY space, the player takes a RALLY card and follows its instructions.
3. Play continues with players taking their turns in order.
4. The winner is the first player to reach the end.

Variations: 1. Put subtraction cards in with the addition cards. For example, "Subtract 3 from each number or the number from 3."

2. Use cards that say "Multiply each number by ____" instead of addition cards.

KEEP YOUR ADDITION IN SHAPE
(2–6 Players)

Preparation

Make a game board, such as the one illustrated in Figure 17, for each player on a twelve-by-twelve-inch piece of railroad board. The numerals and shapes should be arranged differently for each board. Cut 3/4-inch squares of railroad board for markers. Each player needs about fifty. A set of two-by-two-inch cards containing the sums for the 100 addition combinations is also needed. Have an addition table available so players can check answers at the end of a game.

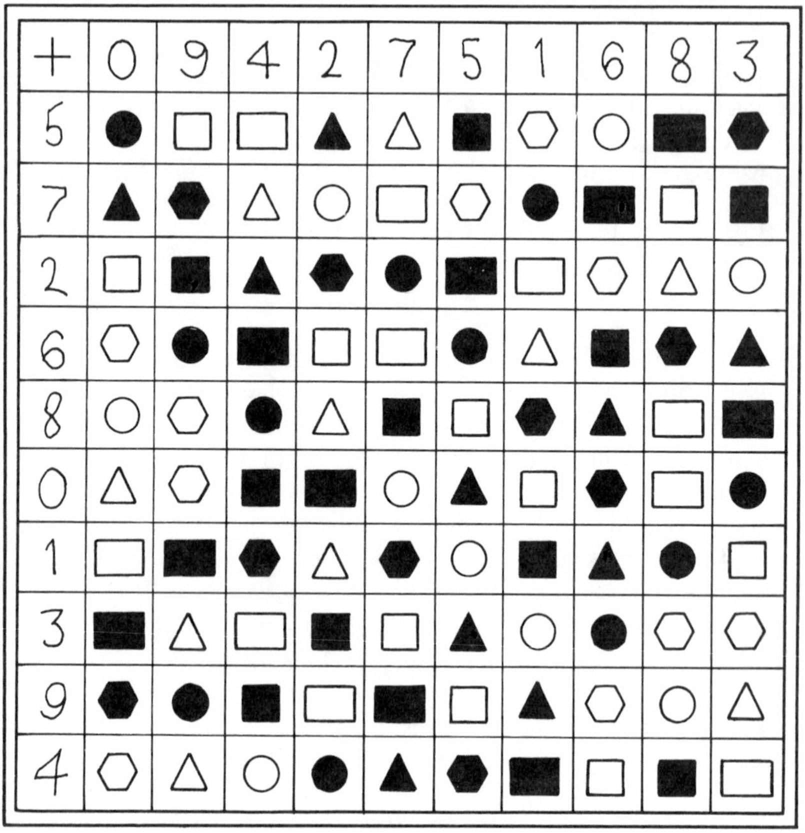

FIGURE 17

Directions

1. Each player has a game board and a set of 3/4-inch squares.
2. The leader mixes the sum cards and puts them face down in a box. He draws one and tells the players what it is.
3. Each player selects a pair of numbers, one from the horizontal row

at the top of the game board and one from the vertical row on the left side of the game board, that equals the sum and puts a marker on his board to cover the shape in the square where the row and column for these numbers meet.

4. The leader draws another sum card and tells what it is.
5. Each player repeats the procedure and again covers a shape on his board. Since the object of the game is to be the first to cover ten squares containing shapes of the same color and kind, a player should check to see if any combinations for the new sum meet at a square containing a shape like the one he first covered. If no such combination exists on his board, he must cover a different shape.
6. Play continues until one player has covered ten shapes of the same color and kind.

DODECAHEDRON ADDITION
(2–4 Players)

Preparation

Make a set of numeral cards for 1 through 12 on twelve three-by-five-inch cards. Make a dodecahedron and number its faces 3 through 14. (A pattern for a dodecahedron is found on page 154 of the Appendix.) Players will need paper and pencil for recording scores.

Directions

1. Put the cards face up and in order where players can reach them easily.
2. The first player rolls the dodecahedron. He tells the number that is on top and picks up a pair of numeral cards containing addends for the number. He continues to roll the dodecahedron and pick up pairs of cards until he rolls a number for which no pair of addends is left. When this happens, he adds the number to those on the remaining numeral cards and records the sum as his score for the round.
3. Play continues with players taking their turns in order until a pre-selected number of rounds are completed or a set amount of time has passed.
4. The winner is the player with the lowest score.

Variations: 1. Let players take single cards in addition to pairs of cards.

2. Let players take as many cards as they want instead of just two.

Given three or more addends less than 20, the student will name their sum.

PLUSSES PAY OFF
(3–6 Players)

Preparation

Make a set of twenty three-by-five-inch cards containing the numerals 1 through 20 for each player. Use a different color for each set. Make another set of sum cards containing the numerals 10 through 50. A few poker chips, or similar objects, are needed.

Directions

1. Each player shuffles his deck of cards and deals himself four. The remaining cards are set aside. The sum cards are shuffled and put face down in a pile. Poker chips—one less than the number of players —are put where each player can reach them.
2. The leader turns over the top sum card and tells what it is.
3. Each player checks his four cards to see if he can add all four and get that sum. If he can, he quietly takes one of the poker chips. As soon as the other players see someone reaching for a chip, they quietly reach for one. The player left without a chip is the loser for the round.
4. If no player has four cards that name the sum, each one passes a card to the player on his left. Again, players check their cards to determine their sum. Players pass cards until someone has four that name the sum for the round.
5. When a player says he has four cards that name the sum, he must put them down and add them. If his answer is correct, he and the other players who got chips score one point each. If his answer is wrong, he must give his point to the player who got none and the other players keep theirs.

6. When a round is over each player reclaims his cards and returns his chip. The sum cards are shuffled and a new one is turned. Each player shuffles and deals himself four more of his cards and play is resumed.
7. The winner is the player with the most chips at the end of a given number of rounds.

PICK YOUR ADDENDS
(2–4 Players)

Preparation

Make a game board for each player (See Figure 18). A game board is a piece of four-by-twenty-eight-inch railroad board separated into

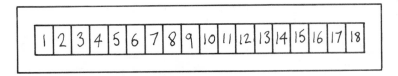

FIGURE 18

eighteen squares. The squares are numbered from 1 through 18. Cut eighteen one-inch squares from railroad board for each player. Three dice are needed.

Directions

1. Each player has a game board and eighteen squares.
2. The first player rolls the dice and counts the number of dots. He puts squares on his board to cover any combination of numbers whose sum equals the number he rolled.
3. Play continues with players taking their turns in order.
4. The game ends when one player covers all his squares. A player must roll the exact number he needs to cover squares on his board. If he cannot play after a roll of the dice he passes for the round.
5. The winner is the first player to cover all of his squares.

Variations: 1. Use only twelve squares numbered from 1 to 12 and two dice.

2. Have players cover the number rolled or only pairs of numbers that equal it.

NUMBER JOIN UP
(2–6 Players)

Preparation

Duplicate game sheets like the one in Figure 19 for each player. Prepare a set of three-by-five-inch cards containing the numerals 10 through 20. Each player also needs a pencil and crayons.

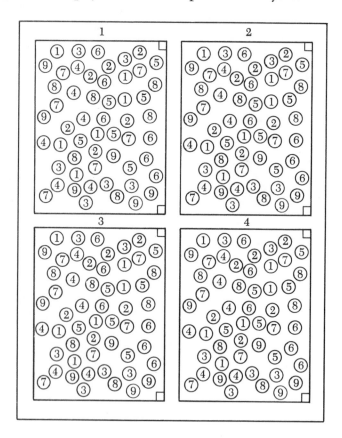

FIGURE 19

Directions

1. Each player has a game sheet, pencil, and some crayons. Put the numeral cards face down in a pile near a player who has been selected to be leader.
2. The leader turns up the top card and tells the number.
3. Each player writes the number's numeral in the box in the upper right-hand corner of the first playing area. He then colors each combination of numbers whose sum equals the game number. For example, if the game number is 15, he can color 8s and 7s; 6s and 9s; three 5s; two 5s, a 4, and a 1; and so on. The object is to color as many combinations as possible. The combinations of *two* addends should be one color; *three* addends, another; *four*, another; and *five* and *six* (if used), other colors. A line of the same color should be drawn to connect the combinations of addends.
4. After each player makes all the combinations of addends he can, he counts them and writes the numeral in the box in the lower right-hand corner of his playing area.
5. The leader draws a second numeral card, and the second round is completed in the second playing area.
6. Play continues until all four playing areas have been used or until a set amount of time has passed.
7. The winner is the player whose total score is the highest.

Given two addends from 100 through 999, the student will name their sum.

ADDITION FOOTBALL
(2 Players)

Preparation

Make a game board that resembles a football field on a piece of twenty-two-by-twenty-eight-inch railroad board (See Figure 20). Cut fifty football-shaped pieces of railroad board for addition combinations.

Mark each one with a pair of addends, each between 99 and 1000. Make two playing pieces in the shape of football players or use plastic players for markers. Make a key so players can check answers during the game.

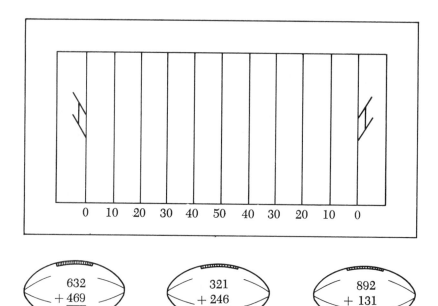

FIGURE 20

Directions

1. Each player puts his marker on the fifty-yard line. One player shuffles the combination cards and puts them face down.

2. The first player takes the top card and reads the addition it contains. He may use paper and pencil, if he wishes, or he can add without them to name the sum. He moves his marker to his opponent's forty-yard line if he names the correct sum. He loses ten yards if his sum is incorrect.

3. Play continues with players alternating moves until one player reaches his opponent's goal line.

4. After a player scores a touchdown he is awarded an extra point if he can name the sum for the next combination card.

5. The players return their markers to the fifty-yard line and resume play after each touchdown.

6. A game can be played by quarters, with a new quarter beginning after one player has scored two touchdowns, or after a set amount of time.

7. The winner is the player who scores the most points.

Variations: 1. Use two numbers between 9 and 100 or larger than 1000.

2. Have both five-yard and ten-yard combination cards. Make the addition on the ten-yard cards more difficult than on the five-yard cards. A player selects the yardage he wants to try for each round.

Commercial games that reinforce addition understanding and skills:

Math Match	Operations Bingo
Heads Up	Triscore
Krypto	Tally
Numble	Big Zero
Tuf	Block It
Sequence	

    (Creative Publications)

ArithmeCubes
I Win
Orbiting the Earth: Addition
    (Scott, Foresman and Company)

Tic Tac Sums
    (A. R. Davis and Co.)

Tumble Numbers
    (Products of the Behavioral Sciences, Inc.)

IMOUT—A Game of Addition and Subtraction
    (IMOUT Arithmetic Drill Games)

ADDO
Imma Whiz—Addition and Subtraction
SUM-UP
Quizmo—Addition and Subtraction

Mathfacts Games
Tri—Ominoes
   (Maries Educational Materials)

Sum Fun
Smarty
   (Gamco Industries, Inc.)

FOO
   (Cuisenaire Company of America)

SUBTRACTION

Given the 100 basic subtraction combinations, the student
will name the differences.

SUBTRACTION TRAIN
(2 Players)

Preparation

Make ten train engines from railroad board. Mark them with the numerals 0 through 9, one numeral to an engine. Make train cars that
have basic subtraction combinations on them. There are ten combinations for 0, ten for 1, through ten for 9. All together there are one hundred combinations. Put pieces of magna tape on the back of each
engine and car. Draw a train track on a magnetic board. Have a subtraction table available so players can check answers during the game.

Directions

1. Mix the engines and put them face down. Put the cars face up and
   mixed near the magnetic board.

FIGURE 21

2. One player turns over an engine card and puts it at the end of the track.
3. The second player picks out all the cars he thinks belong with the engine because their subtraction combinations equal the number on the engine and puts them behind it on the track.
4. Both players check the train to see if the right combinations have been put on. The second player removes all correct cars and keeps them. The players put incorrectly placed cars back to be used again.
5. The winner is the player who has collected the most cars.

Variations: Use addition, multiplication, or division combinations in place of subtraction.

SUBTRACTION TUG OF WAR
(2 Players)

Preparation

Cut masonite to make a board six inches by twenty-seven inches. Cover it with a piece of clear acetate; leave the two ends open. Cut a piece of elastic and make a band to go lengthwise around the board. Attach a button to the band. Out of railroad board cut a "tug of war field" to fit under the plastic and mark it with subtraction combinations. (See Figure 22.) One die is needed.

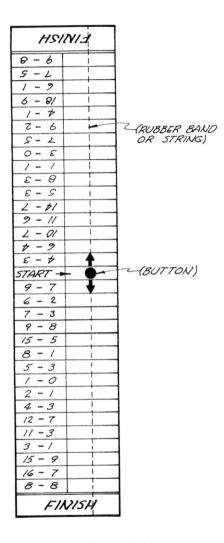

FIGURE 22

Directions

1. Put the "tug of war field" under the acetate and the elastic band around the board with the button over the center line.

2. Each player chooses one end of the board for his goal.

3. The first player rolls the die and moves the button toward his goal the number of spaces indicated. Before he can stay where he stopped he must give the answer to the subtraction combination. Otherwise he must move the button back to the center line.

4. The second player rolls the die and moves the button back toward his goal. He must give the answer to the combination where he stops.

5. Play continues with each player taking his turns in order.

6. The winner is the player who moves the button to his goal first.

Variations: 1. Use addition, multiplication, or division combinations, or a mixture of operations, instead of subtraction.
             2. Use common fractions to rename, decimal fractions to change to percent, or examples from any other areas of mathematics where children need practice.

RED HOT SUBTRACTION
(3–4 Players)

Preparation

Make a game board on a twenty-two-inch square of railroad board, Put a small box in the center of the board for red hot candies. Make a set of at least twenty subtraction combination cards on three-by-five-inch cards. Write combinations for the basic facts you want to practice during the game. Write the answer on another set of three-by-five-inch cards. Make a key so players can check answers during the game. A bag of red hot candy is needed.

Directions

1. Put some red hot candies in the center box.

2. The dealer mixes the two sets of cards and shuffles them. He deals five cards to each player and puts the rest on the game board for a draw pile.

3. The players check their cards for pairs containing a combination and its answer. Each player puts the pairs he has face up on the game board and takes one red hot from the box.

FIGURE 23

4. The players now take turns making matching pairs of cards.
5. The first player selects one of his numeral cards or answer cards and asks one of the other players for a matching card. "I have 6 − 2. Do you have a 4?" Or "I have a 6, do you have a combination card that matches it?" If he gets a card that completes a match, he puts the pair down and takes one red hot. If the player he asks does not have a matching card, he takes the top card from the draw pile. Again, if he makes a match he puts the cards down and takes one red hot. His turn is over after he completes his draw.

6. Play continues with players taking turns in order until one player gets rid of all of his cards.
7. The winner is the player with the most red hots. He wins a bonus of ten red hots.

Variations: Use addition, multiplication, or division for the combination and answer cards.

Given a number smaller than 10 to be subtracted from a number from 10 through 99, the student will name the difference.

SUBTRACTION RING
(2 Players)

Preparation

Make a subtraction ring with an eight-inch diameter from a piece of railroad board. Mark a circle with a two-inch diameter in the center of the ring. Separate the ring into ten sections and mark each with a numeral 0 through 9. Glue a piece of magna-hold paperboard in the center. Cut twenty (or more) circles with two-inch diameters from rail-

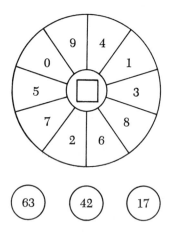

FIGURE 24

road board. Mark each of these with one of the numerals 10 through 99 (See Figure 24). Put a piece of magna tape on the back of each one. Make a key so players can check answers during the game.

Directions

1. Put the numeral cards face down in a small box.
2. Each player draws a numeral card. The one with the larger number plays first.
3. The first player puts his numeral card in the center of the subtraction ring. Then he subtracts each number on the ring from the number in the center. (The other player can use the key to check answers if necessary.) If he gives all ten answers correctly he keeps the numeral card. Otherwise, he returns it to the box.
4. Play continues with players alternately drawing numeral cards and doing the subtraction until all the cards have been used or a set amount of time has passed.
5. The winner is the player who has collected the most numeral cards.

Variation: Have players add the numbers on the ring to the numeral in the center instead of subtracting them.

Commercial games that reinforce subtraction understanding and skills:

Math Match   Tuf
Heads Up   Operations Bingo
Krypto   Triscore
Numble   "Sum" Difference
    (Creative Publications)

ArithmeCubes
I Win
Orbiting the Earth: Subtraction
    (Scott, Foresman and Company)

Tumble Numbers
    (Products of the Behavioral Sciences, Inc.)

IMOUT—A Game of Addition and Subtraction
    (IMOUT Arithmetic Drill Games)

Imma Whiz—Addition and Subtraction

SUM-UP
Quizmo—Addition and Subtraction
Mathfacts Games
Tri-Ominoes
   (Marie's Educational Materials)

Sum Fun
Smarty
   (Gamco Industries Inc.)

FOO
   (Cuisenaire Company of America)

NUMBER LINE

Given a number line containing 0 through 25, the student
will use it to show addition and subtraction.

KANGAROO HOP
(2 Players)

Preparation

Make a playing board similar to the one in Figure 25 on a piece of
eight-by-fifty-six-inch railroad board. (Tape two eight-by-twenty-eight-
inch pieces together to make a strip this long.) Mark three-by-five-inch
cards with these directions (make three of each one): add 1, add 2,
add 3, add 4, add 5, add 6, add 7, add 8, and add 9. Mark each of the
following directions once on three-by-five-inch cards: subtract 1, sub-
tract 2, subtract 3, subtract 4, subtract 5, subtract 6, subtract 7, sub-
tract 8, and subtract 9. Each player needs a marker.

Directions

1. Each player puts his marker on the 0 of the number line. One player
   shuffles the direction cards and puts them face down.

Kangaroo Hop

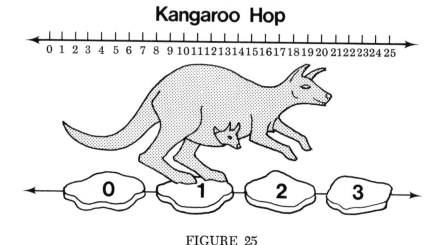

FIGURE 25

2. The first player turns a direction card. If it is an addition card, he adds the number to zero and moves his marker to the point on the line that names the sum. If it is a subtraction card he does not move from 0.

3. The game continues with the players taking their turns in order. Each time a player turns an addition card, he adds the number to the one on which his marker rests on the line. When he turns a subtraction card he subtracts the number from the one on which his marker is.

4. The winner is the player who reaches 25 first.

HORSE RACE
(2–4 Players)

Preparation

Make a race track on a strip of ten-by-fifty-six-inch railroad board. (Tape two ten-by-twenty-eight-inch pieces together to make a strip this long.) Mark it into four lanes and number it as illustrated in Figure 26. Mark a set of twenty-seven three-by-five-inch cards so that eighteen show +1, +2, +3, . . . +9, with two cards for each; and nine show −1, −2, −3, . . . −9. A marker for each player is needed.

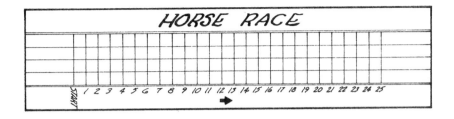

FIGURE 26

Directions

1. Each player puts his marker at the starting line. One player shuffles the addition and subtraction cards and puts them face down.

2. The first player takes the top card and reads what it says. If it is an addition card, he moves his marker along the track the distance it indicates. If it is a subtraction card he waits for his next turn. (A player cannot begin until he gets an addition card.)

3. Play continues with players taking their turns in order. Each time a player draws an addition card, he moves his marker to the right the distance indicated by the sum. He moves it to the left the distance indicated by the difference when he draws a subtraction card.

4. The winner is the player who reaches 25 first.

MULTIPLICATION

Given the 100 basic multiplication combinations, the student will name the products.

MULTIPLICATION HOPSCOTCH
(2–4 Players)

Preparation

Make a playing space for hopscotch with the numerals 0 through 9 in random order. (See Figure 27.) Mark two sets of ten three-by-five-inch cards so they contain 0 through 9, one numeral to a card in each set. Each player needs a stone or small piece of chain to throw.

Directions

1. One player shuffles each set of numeral cards and puts one set face down near HOME and the other at the opposite end.
2. The rules for hopscotch are used.
3. Before a player can begin his hops, he takes the top numeral card. He multiplies the number in each square as he hops across the play-

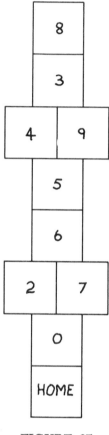

FIGURE 27

ing space by the number named on his card. As long as he names
the right products, he can continue hopping. If he makes a mistake
or cannot name a product, it is a miss, and he must go back to
home and await his next turn.

4. Play continues with players taking their turns in order.

5. The winner is the first person to complete the game.

Variation: Have the numeral cards stand for addends and use addition
        rather than multiplication.

MAGNETIC MULTIPLICATION TABLE
(2–4 Players)

Preparation

Make a playing board on a piece of twenty-two-by-twenty-eight-inch railroad board so that there are 121 squares formed by eleven columns and eleven rows. Put an x (for multiplication) in the upper, left-hand corner. Write the numerals 0 through 9 in the column below and the row next to the x. (See Figure 28.) Put a square-inch piece of magna-hold paperboard in the center of each remaining square. Cut one hundred 1½-inch squares of railroad board for product cards. Mark these so each contains one of the products for a basic multiplication combination. Make four 1½-inch squares and write "wild card" on each one. Put a piece of magna tape on the back of each piece.

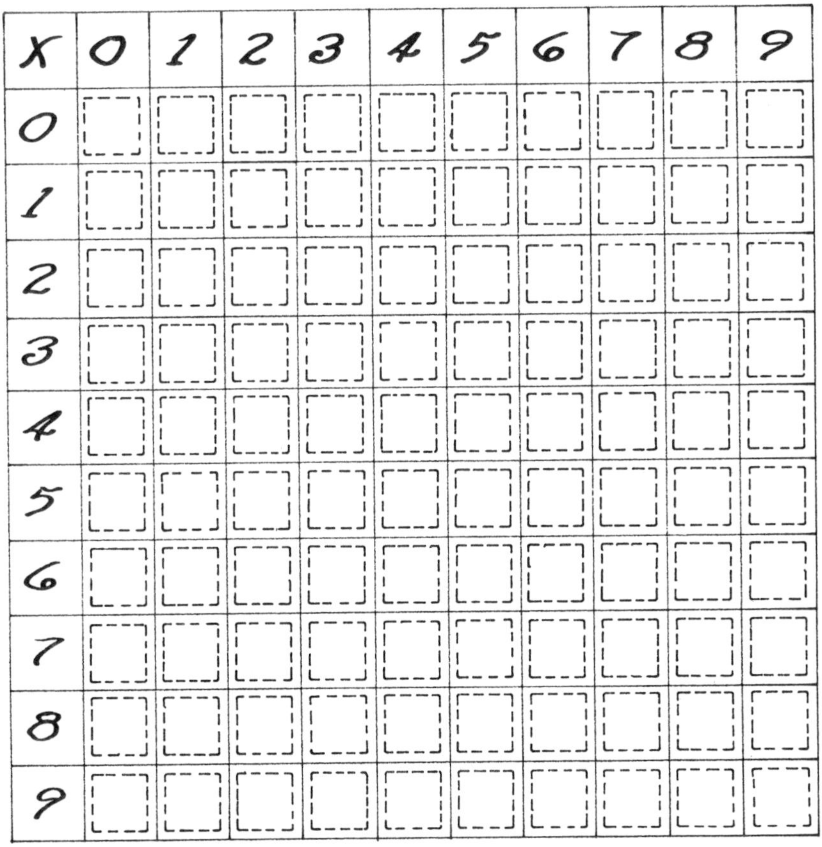

X	0	1	2	3	4	5	6	7	8	9
0										
1										
2										
3										
4										
5										
6										
7										
8										
9										

FIGURE 28

Directions

1. Put the playing board on a bulletin board or in a chalk rail.
2. The players mix the product cards and put them face down near the board.
3. Each player draws seven product cards. A player does not show his cards to his opponents.
4. The first player selects one of his cards and puts it on the playing board in a square where it is the product of the column and row numbers which meet there.
5. The next player has a play if one of his cards can be put in any of the squares that touch the square containing the first product card. For example, if the first player puts a 6 on the board as in Figure 29,

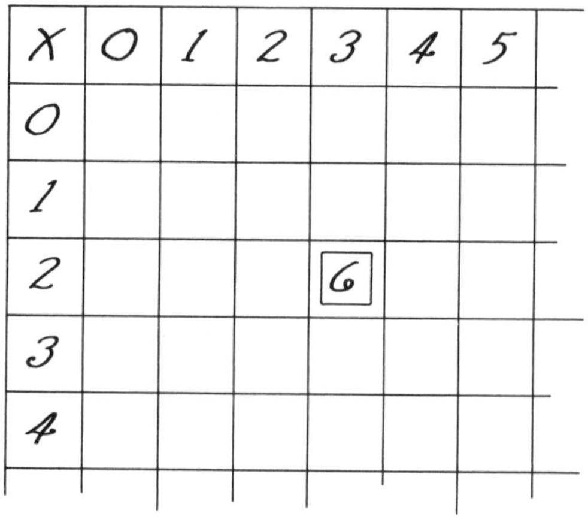

X	O	1	2	3	4	5
O						
1						
2			6			
3						
4						

FIGURE 29

the second player can play any of these products: 2, 3, 4 (two places), 8, 12, 9, or another 6. If he has none of these products, he draws from the face-down cards until he gets one.

6. If a player has a wild card, he can use it instead of drawing product cards, if he wishes. These cards are used to open play in a new part of the game board. If and when a player wants to use a wild card, he shows it to the other players. Then he selects one of his product cards and puts it on the game board. After a wild card has been used it is removed from the game. A player who uses a wild card must draw a replacement for it from the pile of product cards.

7. Play continues with each player taking his turns in order.
8. The winner is the player who gets rid of his cards first.

DEEP SEA DIVE
(2–4 Players)

Preparation

Make a playing board with pictures of a boat, rope ladder, sunken treasure, and underwater creatures and plants on a piece of twenty-two-by-twenty-eight-inch railroad board as shown in Figure 30. Label each

FIGURE 30

rung of the ladder with one of the numerals 0 through 10. Cut ten diving helmets from railroad board. Write one of the numerals 0 through 9 on the back of each. Some small pieces of children's or costume jewelry are needed. Make a key so players can check answers during the game.

Directions

1. Put the helmets face down on the boat and the jewelry on the treasure chest.
2. The first player draws a helmet from the boat. He multiplies the number named on it by each number named on the ladder's rungs. If he reaches the bottom of the ladder he gets to take a piece of jewelry. If he gives a wrong product he must wait for another turn.
3. Play continues with players taking their turns in order.
4. The winner is the player who gets the most pieces of jewelry.

Variation: Use this game for addition instead of multiplication.

Given the product of two numbers, the student will name its factors.

POCKET MULTIPLICATION
(2–5 Players)

Preparation

Make a set of three-by-five-inch cards with the products for the basic multiplication facts you want children to practice. Make a set of twenty factor cards for each child, writing a 0 on the upper half of two of them, 1 on two, through 9 on two. Make a pocket card holder for each player from a six-by-nine-inch piece of railroad board. Fold up two inches of one long side (the bottom width) to make a four-by-nine-inch card holder. Staple each end of the folded strip and points one-third of the way in to make a pocket at each end. Mark an "X" at the upper center of the holder. Prepare an answer key so the leader can check answers during the game. (See Figure 31.)

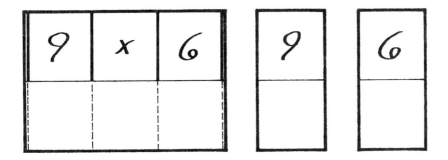

FIGURE 31

Directions

1. Each player has a pocket card holder and a set of factor cards. He arranges his factor cards face up according to number.
2. The leader—a student not playing the game or an aide—shuffles the product cards and shows one.
3. Each player picks up two factor cards which equal this product and puts one in each end of his card holder.
4. The first player to have his cards correctly placed and facing the leader wins a point for the round.
5. The game continues with the leader showing products and the players showing factors until all the product cards have been shown.
6. The winner is the player who earns the most points.

Variation: Use sum and addend cards to make an addition game.

Given a number less than 10, the student will name its multiples under 100.

MULTIPLICATION DOMINOES
(2–5 Players)

Preparation

This game is played with a set of regular dominoes—double six for a simpler game or double nine or twelve for more complex games. In addition, a set of numeral cards 2 through 9 is needed. Players need a paper and pencil for recording scores.

Directions

1. The rules for a standard game of dominoes are used, except that play continues until all dominoes have been used or no more can be played.

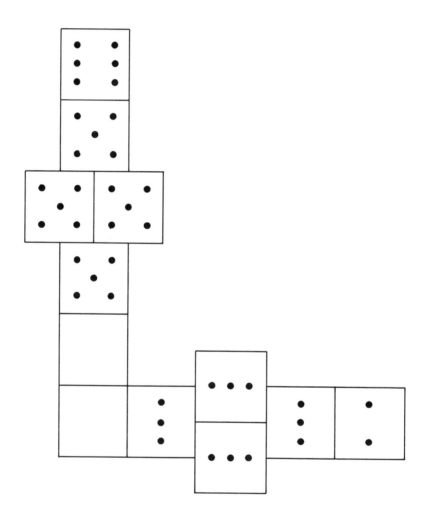

FIGURE 32

2. Turn up the top numeral card to determine the number for which points will be earned during the round. (A round ends after ten dominoes have been played.) For example, if six is the number for a round, each player in turn tries to play a domino so the dots on all the exposed ends total a multiple of six. In Figure 32 the player who put on the domino with the 3 and 2 spots earns 24 points. This score is the sum of the dots on the exposed ends (the six, the double five, the double three and the two).

3. A player records his points each time he makes a multiple of the round's number.

4. After a round has been completed a new numeral card is drawn and a new multiple is used.

5. Play continues with players taking turns in order until all the dominoes have been played.

6. The winner is the player with the most points.

Commercial games that reinforce multiplication understanding and skills:

Math Match	Tuf
Heads Up	Operation Bingo
Krypto	Multifax
Numble	Block It

  (Creative Publications)

ArithmeCubes
I Win
Orbiting the Earth: Multiplication
  (Scott, Foresman and Company)

Divide and Conquer
Tic Tac Times
  (A. R. Davis and Co.)

Tumble Numbers
  (Products of the Behavioral Sciences, Inc.)

IMOUT—A Game of Multiplication and Division
  (IMOUT Arithmetic Drill Games)

SUM-UP
Quizmo—Multiplication and Division

Imma Whiz—Multiplication and Division
(Marie's Educational Materials)

Winning Touch
(Gamco Industries Inc.)

FOO
(Cuisenaire Company of America)

DIVISION

Given the 90 basic division combinations, the student will name the quotients.

DIVISION RUMMY
(2–4 Players)

Preparation

Make a set of twenty-four three-by-five-inch cards that contain division combinations. Make another set of twenty-four cards that contain their quotients. (See Figure 23.) Make a key so players can check answers during the game.

Directions

1. The dealer shuffles the cards and deals seven to each player. He puts the remaining cards face down to make a draw pile and turns up the top card.
2. Players check their cards for combinations and their quotients. All matching pairs are put face up to form number sentences.
3. The first player draws either the top card or one from the draw pile. If he completes a pair he makes a sentence of them. He discards a card and puts it face up beside the draw pile.

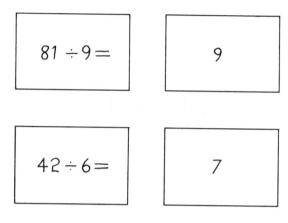

FIGURE 33

4. Play continues with each player taking his turns in order.
5. When a player wants a card below the top card in the discard pile, he can take it only if he takes all the cards above it, too.
6. Play continues until one player is rid of all of his cards.
7. A point is scored for each sentence a player makes.
8. The winner is the player with the most points after a given number of rounds have been completed.

Given two numbers, one not a factor of the other, the student will divide the larger by the smaller and name the quotient and remainder.

ZAP
(2–5 Players)

Preparation

Make a set of sixty three-by-five-inch cards containing division examples having remainders other than zero. (See Figure 34.) Make sixteen ZAP cards. These cards contain statements such as "Remainder < 4," "Remainder is an even number," "Remainder is > than 6."

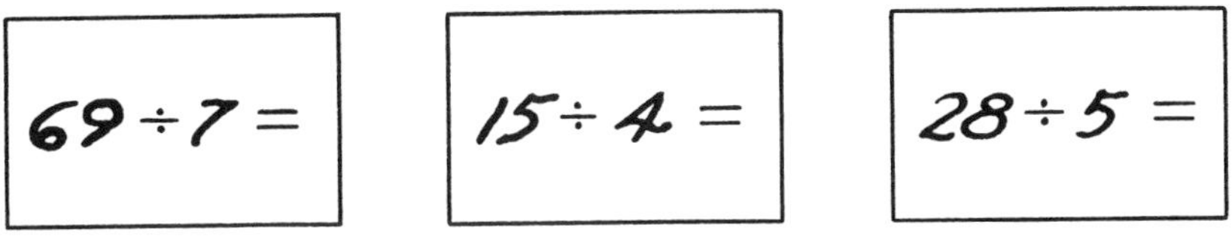

FIGURE 34

Directions

1. The dealer shuffles and deals all the division cards. Each player stacks his, face down. The dealer puts the ZAP cards face down.
2. The dealer turns up the top ZAP card and reads it. The statement on this card guides play during the first round.
3. At a signal from the dealer each player turns up his top card. Players check the turned-up cards to see if any of the remainders match the description on the ZAP card. When there is a match, the first player to say "ZAP" gets all the turned-up cards.
4. The dealer turns up a new ZAP card each time a match is made.
5. Play continues until all players are rid of their cards.
6. The winner is the player who collects the most cards.

NAME THE REMAINDERS
(2–4 Players)

Preparation

Make a game board similar to the one in Figure 35 on a piece of twenty-two-by-twenty-eight-inch railroad board. Make eight cards shaped like roller coaster cars and write one of the numerals 2, 3, 4, . . . 9 on each. Each player will need a marker.

Directions

1. Each player puts his marker in the "start" box. Put the numeral cards face down in their box on the game board.
2. The first player picks up the top numeral card He uses it as a divisor for dividing the first number on the board. For example, if the

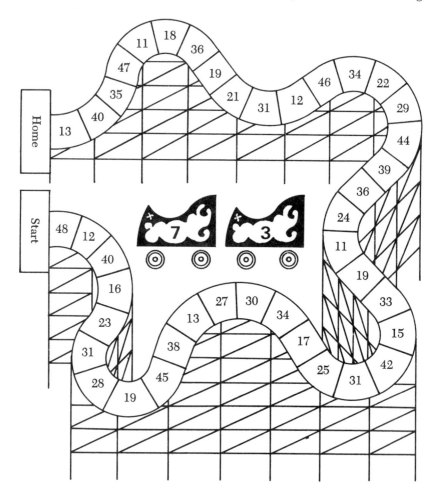

FIGURE 35

numeral he draws is 7, the division is 48 ÷ 7. The player divides and names the remainder. If he names the correct remainder, he moves his marker the number of spaces named by the remainder along the game board. If his answer is incorrect or the remainder is zero, he does not move. The numeral card is put face down at the bottom of the pile.

3. Play continues with each player taking his turns in order.

4. The winner is the player who is first to move around the board.

Variation: Use a die to determine the number of steps a player moves. The player must divide each number as he passes it by the number named on the numeral card he turns over.

Commercial games that reinforce division understanding and skills:

Math Match   Numble
Heads Up   Tuf
Krypto   Rally with Remainders
   (Creative Publications)

ArithmeCubes
I Win
Orbiting the Earth: Division
   (Scott, Foresman and Company)

Divide and Conquer
   (A. R. Davis and Co.)

Tumble Numbers
   (Products of the Behavioral Sciences, Inc.)

IMOUT—A Game of Multiplication and Division)
   (IMOUT Arithmetic Drill Games)

SUM-UP
Quizmo—Multiplication and Division
Imma Whiz—Multiplication and Division
   (Marie's Educational Materials)

FOO
   (Cuisenaire Company of America)

INTEGERS

Given a number line containing both positive and negative integers, the student will identify points to the right of zero as representing positive numbers and points to the left as representing negative numbers.

MOVE TO THE END OF THE LINE
(2 Players)

Preparation

Cut and tape together railroad board to make a six-by-seventy-inch number-line playing board ranging from −20 to 20. Points on the line are 1½ inches apart. (See Figure 36.) Mark twenty three-by-five-inch cards with the numerals 1, 2, 3, . . . 20. Mark twenty cards of another color with the numbers −1, −2, −3, . . . −20.

Directions

1. Put the number line along one edge of a long table or on the floor so two players can sit side by side to play. One player shuffles each deck of cards and puts the positive numbers face down to the right of zero, and the negative numbers to the left of zero.

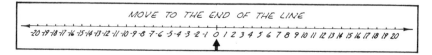

FIGURE 36

2. One player selects 20 as his goal; the other selects −20 as his. Each one sits facing his half of the line. A marker is placed on 0.

3. The positive player turns over his top card and moves the marker to the right as many points as the card's numeral indicates.

4. The negative player turns over his top card and moves the same marker to the left.

5. Play continues with players alternating moves until the marker is moved to either 20 or −20, or beyond. A point is awarded to the player whose goal is reached during the round.

6. The winner is the player with the most points at the end of a given number of rounds.

FUNCTIONS

Given a set of ordered pairs (function), the student will name the rule.

NAME THE OPERATION
(2–4 Players)

Preparation

On three-by-five-inch cards make a deck of cards showing pairs of numerals. A sixty-four card deck will have sixteen sets, each containing four numeral pairs, with one pair to a card. Samples of sets to include are: (3,6) (4,7) (5,8) (6,9); (9,4) (8,3) (7,2) (6,1); (2,8) (3,12) (4,16) (5,20); and (12,6) (10,5) (8,4) (6,3). Make a set of "What's My Rule" cards on a different color of three-by-five-inch cards so there is one for each of the sixteen sets of ordered pairs. Make a key so players can check answers as the game is played.

Directions

1. The dealer shuffles the rule cards and deals four to each player, excluding himself. He puts the ordered pair cards face down.

2. The dealer turns up the top ordered pair card and shows it to the players. If one of them has the rule card to match he says, "I have

77

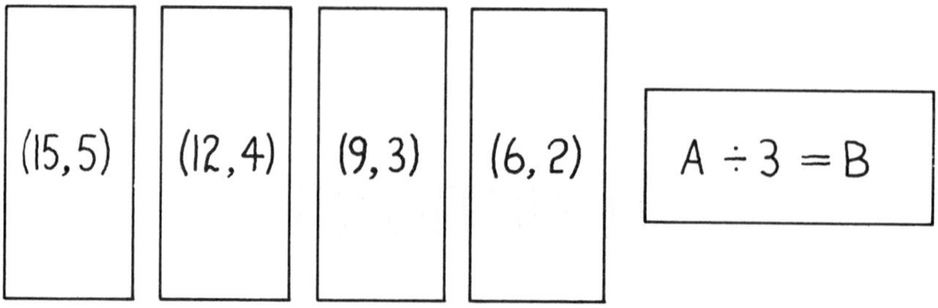

| (15,5) | (12,4) | (9,3) | (6,2) | A ÷ 3 = B |

FIGURE 37

a match." Then he must tell the operation used on the first number of the ordered pair to get the second. If he has a proper match he puts the two cards down in front of himself.

3. Play continues with the dealer showing ordered-pair cards and players matching them.

4. The winner is the first player to match each of his rule cards.

FRACTIONAL NUMBERS

Given a fractional number less than one, the student will make a pictorial representation of it and express it as a common fraction.

DELIVER THE FRACTIONS
(2–4 Players)

Preparation

Make a house for each common fraction the children are studying. (See Figure 38.) Glue a library card pocket to the front of each one. Illustrate the fractions on a set of three-by-five-inch cards. Use regions, line segments, and sets in the illustrations to show each fraction in several ways. (See Figure 39.) Put pictures of the cards that illustrate each fraction on the back of its house so children can check at the end of each game or whenever one player challenges another.

Directions

1. Give each player his share of the cards (called letters) to deliver.
2. The first player shows a card and puts it in the pocket of the correct house.

FIGURE 38

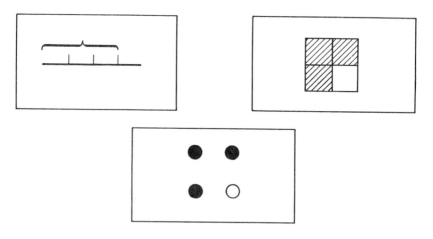

FIGURE 39

3. Play continues with each player delivering his cards in turn.
4. One player may challenge another if he thinks a letter has been improperly delivered. If the challenged player has made an improper delivery he keeps the card and takes all the cards from the pocket of the house to which it should have been delivered. If the challenger is wrong he must take all the cards from the house to which the card was properly delivered.
5. The winner is the player who delivers all of his cards first.

Variations: Put numerals for sums or differences on the houses and addition or subtraction combinations on the cards.

FRACT MATCH
(2–5 *Players*)

Preparation

Prepare a set of three-by-five-inch cards that contains numerals for common fractions—1/2, 1/4, 2/3, 5/6, 7/8, 4/8—and any others with which children are working. Make another set of cards that contains pictures of sets, regions, and line segments separated into parts to represent the common fractions. (See Figure 40.) There should be more than one picture for each fraction card. Make a key so players can check answers during the game.

 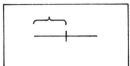 

FIGURE 40

Directions

1. The dealer shuffles the fraction cards and puts them face down. He shuffles the picture cards and deals all of them. Each player puts his picture cards face down in a pile.
2. The dealer turns over the top fraction card.
3. At the dealer's signal each player turns over his top card. If any one or more of the picture cards match the fraction card, the players

say "Fract Match." The first player to say it gets all the picture cards that have been turned up.

4. Play continues with the dealer turning fraction cards and players turning picture cards until all picture cards have been played. (When players turn over their last picture cards without making a match with the top fraction card, each one shuffles his remaining picture cards and puts them face down again so they can continue to play.)

5. The winner is the player who collects the most cards.

Given a fractional number expressed as a common fraction, the student will rename it as a decimal.

DECIMAL TIC-TAC-TOE
(2 Players)

Preparation

Mark a set of three-by-five-inch cards with these common fractions: 1/2, 1/3, 1/4, 1/5, 1/6, 1/8, 1/10, 2/3, 3/4, 2/5, 3/5, 4/5, 5/6, 3/8, 5/8, 7/8, 3/10, 7/10, 9/10. A regular or three-dimensional tic-tac-toe board and markers are needed. Make a key so players can check answers during play.

Directions

1. One player shuffles the fraction cards and puts them face down.

2. The first player turns over the top card and renames the common fraction as a decimal fraction. If his answer is correct he puts a marker on the tic-tac-toe board. Otherwise, his turn is over.

3. Play continues with each player taking his turns in order.

4. The winner is the player who gets three markers in a row on the tic-tac-toe board.

Variation: Use decimal fraction cards and have players change the decimals to common fractions or percent.

COMMON DECIMAL FRACTION SAFARI
(2–4 Players)

Preparation

Make a game board on a piece of twenty-two-by-twenty-eight-inch railroad board. The board in Figure 41 has a jungle safari theme. The steps

FIGURE 41

along the trail are marked consecutively with decimal notation. The safari and scene spaces are included in the count but are not numbered. Cut eighteen two-by-three-inch cards from railroad board and write "SAFARI" on them. The Safari cards contain these directions:

> Your camera is broken. Go back 3 spaces for repairs.
> Your water supply is running low. Go to the water hole for more.
> You dropped the map. Go back 2 spaces to pick it up.
> You became lost in the jungle. Go back 3 spaces to get back on the trail.
> The elephant herd is near the trail. Go there to see it.
> There's a little monkey in the tree up there. Go ahead 2 spaces to see it.
> The herd of zebras is ready to be photographed. Go to them for your pictures.
> The waterfall is beautiful. You haven't seen it yet, so go there now.
> The raft is across the river. Lose a turn while you wait for it.
> The rain is coming down hard. Lose a turn while you wait for it to stop.
> The radio is broken. Lose a turn while it's repaired.
> Lunch is being served in camp. Go there to eat.
> You kept the supplies from going under when the canoe overturned. Take an extra turn.
> You took time to pack the gear. Take an extra turn.
> You repaired the truck's engine. Take an extra turn.
> You need some medicine. Go ahead 3 spaces to get it.
> You see a chimpanzee beside the trail. Move ahead 4 spaces to get its picture.
> You want a picture of lions. Go to them to take it.

A pair of dice, one red and one green, and a marker for each player are needed.

Directions

1. Each player puts his marker on the game board at the Safari's beginning.
2. The first player rolls the dice. He reads the red one for the numerator of a common fraction and the green one for its denominator. Once he names the common fraction shown by the dice he changes it to a decimal fraction. (He may divide the numerator by denominator using paper and pencil if he wishes.) Each decimal

fraction is named to the nearest tenth. The player moves his marker the number of tenths his number indicates.

3. When a player stops on a Safari space he takes a Safari card and follows its instructions.
4. Play continues with each player taking his turns in order.
5. The winner is the player who reaches the end first.

Given a fractional number expressed as a common fraction with a numerator of 1 and denominator less than 10, the student will tell how many there are in 1.

SPINNER FRACTIONS
(2–6 Players)

Preparation

Cut a set of six geometric shapes from railroad board for each player. Make a circle with a five-inch diameter and polygons with three to six-inch edges. Cut each shape into parts as shown in Figure 42. Make a playing board for each player. A playing board contains an outline of each cut-out shape. Make a six-part spinner with one of the common fractions 1/2, 1/3, 1/4, 1/5, 1/6 and 1/8 named on one of the six parts. (Directions for making a spinner are on page 147 of the Appendix.)

Directions

1. Each player has a set of cut-up shapes and a playing board.
2. The first player spins and names the fraction on which the spinner stops. He takes a piece of one of the cut-up shapes the size of the fraction and puts it on his playing board. If he wants, he may play a combination of pieces equivalent to the fraction.
3. Play continues with players taking their turns in order.
4. The winner is the player who fills the outlines on his playing board first or who has the most covered at the end of a given period of time.

Variation: Use an octahedron instead of polygon spinner. Use 2/3 and 3/4 along with the common fractions named for the spinner.

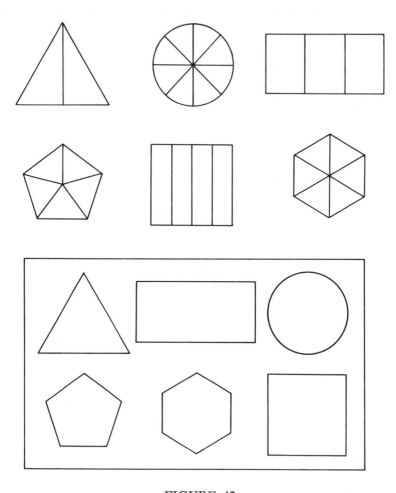

FIGURE 42

SIMPLE SIMON'S PIES
(2-4 Players)

Preparation

Make a game board on a piece of twenty-two-by-twenty-eight-inch railroad board. (See Figure 43.) Cut the path of circles from a neutral color of railroad board and glue them on the game board. Color a fractional part of each one black. Make a response board for each

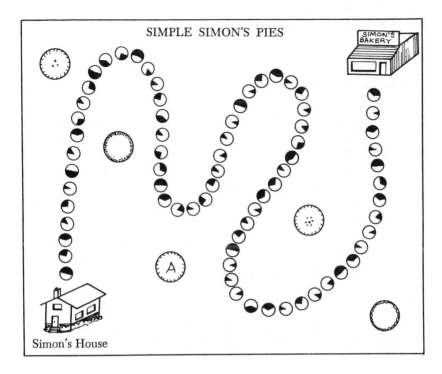

FIGURE 43

player like the one in Figure 44. Make the circles with a five-inch diameter. Cut a set of four circles with five-inch diameters from colored railroad board for each response board. Use red to represent a cherry pie, green for apple, yellow for lemon, and blue for blueberry. Cut

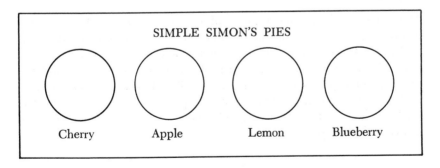

FIGURE 44

one of these into halves, another into thirds, another fourths, and the last eighths. A die and a marker are needed for each player.

Directions

1. Each player has a response board and a set of five-inch fractional pieces.
2. The first player rolls the die and moves his marker the number of spaces indicated. When he completes his move he names the size of the piece of pie on which he stops. Then he takes a fractional piece of the same size (or pieces equivalent to it) and puts it on any one of the circles on his response board.
3. Play continues with each player taking his turns in order until one player reaches the end.
4. The players determine what part of their pies are covered and each one names the mixed fraction that tells the total amount he covered.
5. The winner is the player who covers the most pies.*

Given two fractional numbers smaller than 1 expressed as common fractions, the student will name their sum.

COMMON FRACTION ADDITION
(2 Players)

Preparation

Make a game board on a piece of twenty-two-by-twenty-eight-inch railroad board. The small squares on each side of the common fractions in Figure 45 are pieces of magna-hold paperboard to hold sentence cards. Make two identical sets of sentence cards, one on red and the other on blue pieces of 2-by-4½-inch railroad board, which indicate addition of common fractions. Put two pieces of magna tape on the back of each card. A die is needed. Make a key so players can check answers as they play.

---

*We thank Mary Wohlers for this game.

RED				BLUE			
☐ $\frac{1}{2}$ ☐	☐ $\frac{7}{8}$ ☐	☐ $\frac{3}{7}$ ☐	☐ $\frac{3}{4}$ ☐
☐ $\frac{2}{3}$ ☐	☐ $\frac{3}{5}$ ☐	☐ $\frac{4}{8}$ ☐	☐ $\frac{4}{5}$ ☐
☐ $\frac{3}{4}$ ☐	☐ $\frac{2}{7}$ ☐	☐ $\frac{1}{2}$ ☐	☐ $\frac{6}{7}$ ☐
☐ $\frac{5}{8}$ ☐	☐ $\frac{6}{7}$ ☐	☐ $\frac{3}{8}$ ☐	☐ $\frac{4}{7}$ ☐
☐ $\frac{7}{6}$ ☐	☐ $\frac{6}{8}$ ☐	☐ $\frac{1}{4}$ ☐	☐ $\frac{2}{3}$ ☐
☐ $\frac{2}{5}$ ☐	☐ $\frac{2}{4}$ ☐	☐ $\frac{6}{7}$ ☐	☐ $\frac{2}{8}$ ☐
☐ $\frac{1}{4}$ ☐	☐ $\frac{5}{7}$ ☐	☐ $\frac{7}{6}$ ☐	☐ $\frac{3}{7}$ ☐
☐ $\frac{6}{7}$ ☐	☐ $\frac{4}{8}$ ☐	☐ $\frac{2}{5}$ ☐	☐ $\frac{5}{8}$ ☐
☐ $\frac{5}{6}$ ☐	☐ $\frac{4}{5}$ ☐	☐ $\frac{3}{8}$ ☐	☐ $\frac{4}{7}$ ☐
☐ $\frac{3}{5}$ ☐	☐ $\frac{5}{8}$ ☐	☐ $\frac{6}{7}$ ☐	☐ $\frac{2}{5}$ ☐
☐ $\frac{2}{8}$ ☐	☐ $\frac{2}{7}$ ☐	☐ $\frac{6}{8}$ ☐	☐ $\frac{2}{4}$ ☐
☐ $\frac{3}{5}$ ☐	☐ $\frac{2}{3}$ ☐	☐ $\frac{5}{7}$ ☐	☐ $\frac{7}{8}$ ☐

$\frac{1}{4} + \frac{1}{4}$	$\frac{1}{3} + \frac{1}{3}$	$\frac{1}{2} + \frac{1}{4}$	$\frac{1}{4} + \frac{3}{8}$

FIGURE 45

Directions

1. Put the game board on a bulletin board or in a chalk rail. Each player has a set of sentence cards.
2. The first player rolls the die. The number he rolls tells how many sentence cards he can put on the game board. He selects any of

his cards and puts them up on his side of the board next to the appropriate sum.

3. An opponent may challenge any play. If a player has made an incorrect play, the challenger gets to play as many of his cards as the other player had left to play. If a challenger is wrong, the player gets to play as many extra cards as the number he had left to play.

4. Play continues with players alternating turns until one player is rid of his cards.

5. The winner is the player who is rid of his cards first.

ADD TO MAKE ONE
(2–4 Players)

Preparation

A pair of dice—one red and one green—and paper and pencil for recording scores are all the equipment needed. Make an answer key so players can check answers during play.

Directions

1. The player who has been chosen leader rolls the dice. The red die names a numerator while the green die names a denominator.

2. The first player names the fraction indicated by the dice. Then he names another fraction that can be added to it to give a sum of 1. If he is correct, he scores one point.

3. Play continues with each player taking his turns in order.

4. The winner is the player who has the most points after a given number of rounds have been played or a given period of time has passed.

Given a common fraction representing a fractional number less than 1, the student will name common fractions equivalent to it.

MONSTER FRACTIONS
(3–5 Players)

Preparation

Make a set of three-by-five-inch fraction cards using these common fractions: 1/2, 3/6, 1/4, 2/8, 1/5, 2/10, 1/3, 2/6, 1/6, 2/12, 1/7, 3/21, 1/8, 2/16, 2/2, 1, 3/8, 6/16, 2/5, 6/15, 2/3, 8/12, 3/5, 6/10, 5/6, 10/12, 2/7, 4/14, 3/7, 6/14, 4/7, 12/21, 5/7, 10/14, 6/7, 18/21, 5/8, 10/16, 7/16, 21/24, 4/5, 12/15, 3/4, 9/12, 3/2, 1-1/2, 4/3, 1-1/3, 5/4, 1-1/4, 4/2, 2, 7/5, 1-2/5, 5/3, 1-2/3, 11/8, 1-3/8. Make one "monster card" on a three-by-five-inch card of the same color and an answer key to show the equivalent fractions in the set, e.g., 1/2 = 3/6, 1/4 = 2/8. (See Figure 46.)

Directions

1. The dealer shuffles the cards and deals them.

FIGURE 46

2. Each player checks his cards for pairs that are equivalent fractions and lays these down.
3. The first player takes a card from the hand of the player on his right. If the new card is the equivalent of one in his hand he discards the pair. If he has no match he puts the new card in his hand.
4. Play continues with each player drawing in turn from the player on his right and putting down matching pairs.
5. When a player rids his hand of his cards he is out of the game for the rest of the round.
6. Each player who gets rid of all of his cards is a winner. The loser is the player who holds the monster card at the round's end.

Variations: 1. Use only common fractions that name fractional numbers equal to or greater than one.
2. Use common fractions and their equivalent decimal fractions to make the matching pairs.

Given two fractional numbers expressed as decimal fractions, the student will name their sum or difference.

DECIMAL TRACK MEET
(2–4 Players)

Preparation

Make a game board on a piece of twenty-two-by-fifty-six-inch railroad board. (Tape two pieces of twenty-two-by-twenty-eight-inch railroad board together.) The squares to the left of the starting line and the strips down each lane of the track are magna-hold paperboard. (See Figure 47.) Make a set of playing cards containing decimal fraction addition and subtraction combinations. Each player needs a magnetic marker. Make a key so players can check answers during play.

1. Put the game board on a bulletin board or in a chalk rail. One player shuffles the playing cards and puts them face down. Each player puts his marker on the board to the left of the starting line.
2. The first player takes the top playing card. He names the sum or difference and moves his marker as many tenths as the answer indicates. If an opponent challenges an answer and is correct, the

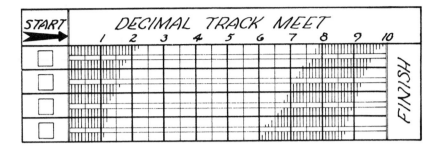

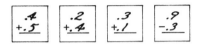

FIGURE 47

player does not move his marker. If a challenge is made incorrectly, the challenger loses his next turn.

3. Play continues with each player taking his turns in order.
4. The winner is the player who reaches the finish line first.

DECIMAL DIFFERENCE
(2–4 Players)

Preparation

Make a set of sentence cards on three-by-five-inch cards. Each card contains a subtraction sentence involving fractional numbers expressed as decimal fractions, like those in Figure 48. Write the sentence and its answer on the back of each card. Make a pocket card holder with two pockets and a set of response cards for each player. The response cards should contain two cards for each of the numbers 0 through 9. A pencil and paper for recording scores are needed.

Directions

1. The leader, who is not a player, shuffles the sentence cards and keeps them out of the players' sight.

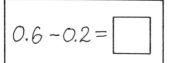

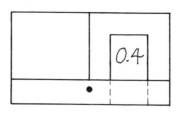

FIGURE 48

2. Each player has a pocket card holder and a set of answer cards.
3. The leader shows the top sentence card. Each player determines the answer and records it with answer cards in his pocket holder.
4. The first player to show the leader the correct answer gets a point for the round.
5. Play continues with the leader showing sentence cards and players showing their answers.
6. The winner is the player with the most points after all sentence cards have been shown or a given amount of time has passed.

Variations: 1. Have addition sentences instead of subtraction.
2. Have multiplication and division sentences. Use a three-pocket card holder to show hundredths as well as tenths.

Commercial games that reinforce understanding of fractional numbers and ways they are represented:

One
Recognizing Fractional Parts
(Creative Publications)

IMOUT—a Game of Fractions
(IMOUT Arithmetic Drill Games)

Fractions Are As Easy As Pie
  (Marie's Educational Materials)

Frac Pac
  (A. R. Davis and Co.)

MEASUREMENT

Given a ruler and chalk, the student will measure distances to twelve inches using inch and half-inch units.

BLAST OFF
(2–4 Players)

Preparation

For each player, cut a rocket, a moon, and a launching pad from rail-road board. Mark and number the rockets as shown in Figure 49. Put pieces of magna tape on the back of each of these pieces. Each player needs a large magnetic board, a ruler marked in inches, and a piece of chalk.

Directions

1. Each flight begins with tails of the rockets against the launching pads, which are placed at the left edge of the magnetic board.
2. The player with the number 1 rocket rolls and counts the number of dots on both dice. He measures from the tip of his rocket the number of inches indicated by the dice and makes a mark on the magnetic board. He moves the rocket so its point is at the mark.

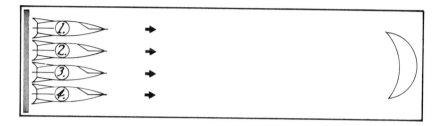

FIGURE 49

3. Play continues with each player taking his turns in order.
4. The winner is the player whose rocket reaches the moon first.

GRAND PRIX
(2 Players)

Preparation

Tape two sheets of railroad board together to make a twenty-two-by-fifty-six-inch race track. Mark a starting line at one end, a finish line at the other, and a dividing line down the middle. (See Figure 50.) Cut forty-six two-by-three-inch cards from railroad board. Mark five cards with "Pit Stop" and a black flag on the same side. Mark a red flag and one of the measurements 1 in., 2 in., 3 in., . . . 12 in. on the same side of twelve. Mark a green flag on five. Mark the measurements (by ½ inch) ½ in., 1 in., 1½ in. . . . 12 in. on the remaining twenty-four. Each player needs a toy race car and ruler marked in half inches.

Directions

1. Two drivers race at a time. Each race begins with the nose of the cars lined up at the starting line.
2. One player shuffles the cards and puts them face down on the floor.
3. The first player picks up a card. If the card has a measurement and no flag on it, he moves ahead as far as the measurement says. If the card has a red flag and a measurement on it, he does not move from the starting line. Later, when he draws such a card he will move backward the distance the measurement says (or back to the start, if he is too near it to go back the full distance). If he draws a green

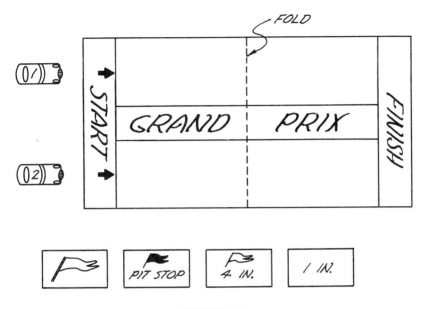

FIGURE 50

flag card he gets another turn. If he draws a black flag card he loses a turn.

4. Each measurement is to be taken from the nose of a car.
5. The winner is the player whose car reaches the finish line first.

Given a ruler and objects to measure, the student will measure them using inch and half-inch units.

MOUSE HOUSE
(2–4 Players)

Preparation

Cut a three-sided mouse house from railroad board for each player. (See Figure 51.) Glue eight library pockets to the panels of each house. Write a measurement—2″, 3″, . . . 9″—on each pocket. Also cut for each player eight mice from railroad board. Cut and glue to each mouse a tail of yarn or string as long as one of the measurements. Cut a small square from each of eight different colors of railroad board and glue one to each mouse. Make an octahedron. (Directions for making an octahedron are on page 153 of the Appendix.) Color each face of the octahedron to match one of the colors of the railroad board squares. Each player needs a ruler marked in inches.

Directions

1. Each player has a mouse house, eight mice, and a ruler.
2. The first player rolls the octahedron. He picks up the mouse with

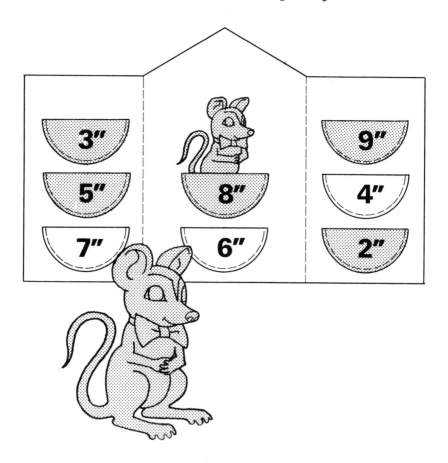

FIGURE 51

the colored square that matches the color on the "up" face. He measures its tail and puts the mouse in its appropriate pocket in the house.

3. The game continues with players taking their turns in order.

4. When a player has no mouse to match the color on the octahedron he has no play for the round.

5. The winner is the player who fills his mouse house pockets first.

WORMY APPLES BINGO
(2-4 Players)

Preparation

Cut thirty-six apples with four-inch diameters from railroad board. Glue a leaf and stem to each one. Write one of the measurements: 1",

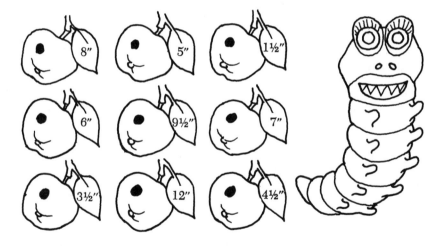

FIGURE 52

1½", 2", 2½" . . . 12" on each stem. (See Figure 52.) Cut worm holes from black railroad board and glue one to each apple, putting the glue around the side and bottom edges of the worm holes so the top is open to let a worm in. Cut twenty-three five-inch worms and glue a piece of yarn or string the length of one of the measurements on the apples to the tail of each one. Make nine smaller worms for each player to use as markers. Each player needs a ruler.

Directions

1. Arrange nine apples in a three-by-three array on a bulletin board or wall for each player. The set is large enough to make four nine-apple arrays. Give each player nine small worms.

2. Put the larger worms in a box where each player can reach them easily.

3. The first player takes a worm from the box, measures its tail, and tells its measurement. The players who have the measurement on one of the apples in their arrays put a small worm in the worm hole. (More than one person may have a measurement since some of the numbers are repeated on the apples.)

4. Play continues with players taking turns drawing worms and measuring their tails until one player has worms in three apples across a row, down a column, or through a diagonal.

WHAT'S MY MEASURE?
(2–6 Players)

Preparation

Make a set of problem cards on three-by-five-inch cards. On each one write a problem such as, "I am the door to your classroom. How many inches wide am I?" "I am the shelf holding the dictionaries. How many inches above the floor am I?" "I am the 'A' encyclopedia. How many inches wide am I?" Rulers, yard sticks, and a piece of paper and pencil for each player are needed.

Directions

1. The cards are put face down. One at a time, they are turned over. The players take turns reading the cards as they are turned.

2. After a card has been read each player makes an estimate of the answer and writes it down.

3. The players measure the objects after all the estimates have been made and check their answers against the measurements.

4. The winner is the player who has made the most estimates nearest the actual measurements.

Given a set of real or toy money containing coins and dollar bills, the student will use them to make imaginary purchases and to make change.

BUY THE TOYS
(3–4 Players)

Preparation

Cut out or draw pictures of simple toys or use small plastic whistles, cars, animals and put each one on a three-by-five-inch card. Mark a price for each toy on its card, e.g., whistle—3 cents. Make a toy shop on a piece of twenty-two-by-twenty-eight-inch railroad board. Glue

FIGURE 53

twelve library pockets on the face of the store. (See Figure 53.) A set of toy money with coins to twenty-five cents is also needed.

Directions

1. One player serves as the shopkeeper. The others are buyers. Each buyer has up to fifty cents in coins.

2. The salesman points to a toy. One of the players names its price and counts out enough coins to pay for it. If he names the correct price and gives the shopkeeper the right coins, he keeps the toy.

3. The game continues with the players taking their turns in order.

4. The winner is the player who has the most toy cards.

HOW CAN I PAY FOR IT?
(2–4 Players)

Preparation

Make a set of three-by-five-inch cards picturing objects and their prices: doll—59 cents, car—45 cents, and so on. One three-minute egg timer and boxes containing many toy or real coins are needed. (See Figure 54.)

Directions

1. The toy cards are put face down. One player serves as leader to turn them over. Each player has a box of coins.

2. The leader turns over a card and reads its price. At the same time he starts the egg timer.

3. Each player has three minutes to arrange as many combinations of coins equaling the object's price as he can. A player scores one point for each correct combination. A player's combinations should be checked by the other players before they are accepted.

4. The game continues with the leader turning cards and players making combinations until all the cards have been turned or a set amount of time has passed.

5. The winner is the player who has earned the most points.

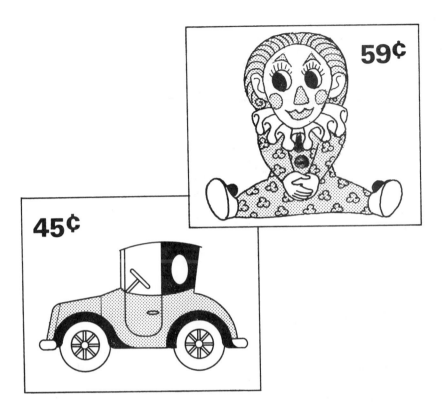

FIGURE 54

SHOPPING SPREE
(3–5 Players)

Preparation

Make a large purse from railroad board for each player. Glue two strips of magna-hold paperboard to the front of each one. Put pieces of magna tape on the back of coins and bills from a set of toy money. Use three-by-five-inch cards to illustrate objects for sale and their prices. Picture objects and prices according to your childrens' level of understanding of money. (See Figure 55.) A piece of paper and pencil are needed for each player.

Directions

1. One child serves as leader. The others are shoppers.

FIGURE 55

2. The leader starts a round by putting coins—and a bill perhaps—on each of the purses. He gives a purse to each player. He shuffles the cards and shows one.

3. Each player determines if he has enough money to buy the pictured object. If he has, he determines the change he will get. If not, he figures how much more money he needs to pay for it. Either way, he scores a point if he is correct. Each player's answer should be checked by the leader and other players before it is accepted.

4. The game continues with the leader putting money on the purses and showing cards.

5. The winner is the player who earns the most points.

PAY THE BANKER
(2–4 Players)

Preparation

Make a large dollar sign on a piece of eighteen-by-twenty-two-inch railroad board. Divide the dollar sign into squares writing amounts of money in some of the squares as in Figure 56. Cut twelve pieces of two-by-three-inch railroad board for direction cards. Mark a dollar sign on one side and one of these directions on the other side of each of the cards:

You share your money with friends. Pay everyone 12¢
Your dog got loose. You are fined. Pay 17¢
Gasoline taxes must be paid. Pay 26¢

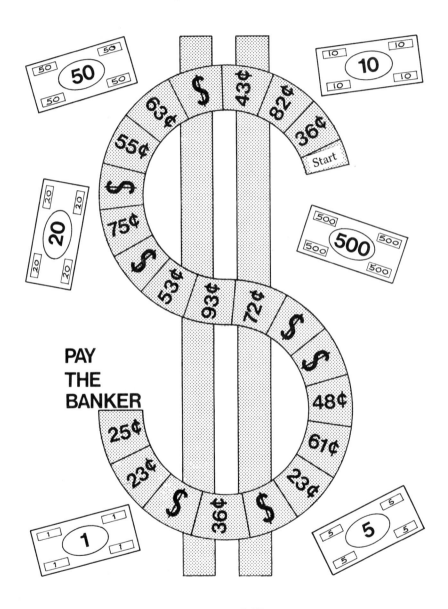

FIGURE 56

You found some money and get a reward. Collect 67¢
Property taxes are due today. Pay 58¢
You must license your bicycle. Pay 27¢
You caught the bank robber. Collect 52¢
Your savings earn you interest. Collect 45¢
Fire insurance is due. Pay 39¢
Interest on your loan is due today. Pay 43¢
Sales tax on new roller skates. Pay 18¢
You mow the lawn. Collect 50¢

A set of toy money containing coins and dollar bills, a die, and a marker for each player are needed.

Directions

1. One player is selected to serve as banker. He gives each player a dollar bill to begin play. Each player puts his marker on the Start square. The dollar cards are put face down on the board.

2. The first player rolls the die and moves his marker. If he stops on a space marked with an amount of money, he collects from the banker. If he lands on a space marked with a dollar sign, he takes a card and follows its directions.

3. Play continues with each player taking his turns in order until all players have reached the end.

4. A player who runs out of money before he reaches the end may borrow from the banker, if he wishes. (Whether or not he borrows money will depend upon how far he is on the board and how much money other players have.)

5. The winner is the player with the most money after all have reached the end. (A player who borrows money must repay his loan before he figures the amount of money he has.)

Given a clock or picture of one showing time to the quarter hour, the student will name the time and express it using words, e.g., 12 o'clock, and symbols, e.g., 12:00.

IT'S BASEBALL TIME
(2, 4, or 6 Players)

Preparation

Cut twenty-five four-inch circles from railroad board for baseballs. Write a time, such as 12 o'clock on one side and draw a clock face showing the time on the other side of each ball. The complete set will contain clocks showing times to the hour, half hour, and quarter hour. Cut an eighteen-inch square of railroad board and draw a baseball diamond on it. Nine plastic ball players are needed for each team. (See Figure 57.)

Directions

1. The game is played by two teams, each having one, two, or three players.

2. The teams face each other at a table, with the ball diamond between them and the balls stacked on one side with the clock faces up. One team is selected to bat first; the other is in the field. Each team has nine plastic ball players for markers. The first batter puts a marker on home plate.

3. A player from the team in the field holds up a ball with the clock face toward the batter. The batter tells the time it shows. The pitcher—the player who holds the baseball—checks the back of the ball to see if the answer is correct. If it is correct, the batter moves his marker to first base.

4. The next player puts a plastic player on home plate. He is shown another clock. If he answers correctly, the first batter moves his marker to second base while the second batter moves his to first base.

5. Play continues with players moving their pieces around the bases each time a correct answer is given. An out is made for each incorrect answer. A run is scored after a team gives four correct answers and moves a marker across home plate. Each correct answer after four scores another run until a team makes three outs.

6. Each team is responsible for keeping its own score.

7. Play continues until each team has had an equal number of half innings at bat.

8. The winning team is the one that scores the most points. (Add new clock faces as children extend their study to times not included in the original set.)

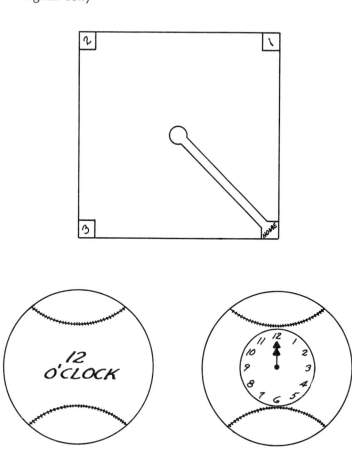

FIGURE 57

ON TIME

(2–5 Players)

Preparation

Cut five eight-by-ten-inch cards from railroad board. Draw four 2½-inch clock faces (leave the hands off) on a spirit duplicating master. Hand feed the railroad board through the duplicating machine to make four faces on each one. Cut them to make four four-by-five-inch clock-face cards. Draw hands on each clock to show a different time to the hour or half hour. Cut forty four-by-five-inch cards from railroad board. Write the time for each clock face using words on twenty and numerals on the other twenty. (See Figure 58.)

Directions

1. The dealer shuffles the cards and deals five to each player. He puts the remaining cards face down and turns up the top card.

4:00
4 o'clock

7:30
Seven thirty

FIGURE 58

2. The player to the dealer's left has the first play. If he has three cards that show the same time, he puts them face up in front of him. Each time a player puts down three cards he replaces them in his hand with the top three cards from the draw pile. If a player has no cards to lay down, he takes the top card from the draw pile or the turned-up card. If the card he draws gives him a three-card match, he puts the cards down and replaces them from the draw pile. Otherwise, he discards the card he drew or puts it in his hand and discards another.

3. Play passes to the next player, who puts down any matches he holds. He completes his play by replacing cards played from his hand or making a draw and discard.

4. Play continues with each player taking his turns in order until one player is rid of all of his cards. If players go through the draw pile before anyone gets rid of his cards, the dealer shuffles the discards, puts them face down, and turns up the top card so play can continue.

5. The winner is the player who has completed the most sets of matching cards.

Given a region enclosed by line segments, the student will measure and name its area.

AREA FILL UP
(2–4 Players)

Preparation

Make a game board like the one in Figure 59 for each player. Each game board is made on a piece of fourteen-by-twenty-two-inch railroad board. The sides of each shape are measured in whole inches. Cut a set of shapes for each player as in Figure 59. The number below each shape tells how many of each to make. A die is needed.

Directions

1. Each player has a game board and a set of shapes.
2. The first player rolls the die. The number it shows tells how many

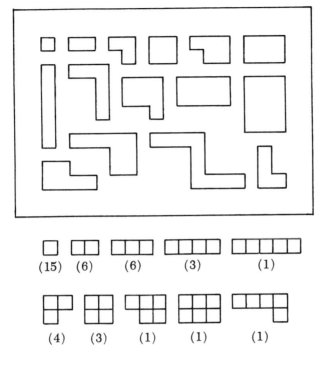

(15)   (6)   (6)   (3)   (1)

(4)   (3)   (1)   (1)   (1)

FIGURE 59

units he can put on his game board during the round. He selects any combination of shapes he wants and fits them into a region or regions on his board. (Once a player puts a piece on his board he cannot move it.)

3. The game continues with each player taking his turns in order.

4. The winner is the player who fills his board first. Before he can claim a win he must first name the number of squares in each region.

Commercial games that reinforce understanding of measurement:

Spin-A-Coin
Spin-A-Gallon
Liquid Measure Game
    (Creative Publications)

Pay the Cashier
Count Your Change
Quizmo—Tell Time
  (Marie's Educational Games)

PROBABILITY

Given a die, the student will determine the probabilities for rolling an odd number and an even number.

ODD-EVEN RACE
(2 Players)

Preparation

Make a playing board similar to the one in Figure 60 on a piece of twenty-two-by-twenty-eight-inch railroad board. Each player needs a die, score sheet, and marker.

Directions

1. Each player puts his marker at the starting place.
2. One player rolls the die to decide whether he will take the even or the odd track of the board.
3. Either player rolls the die to start the game. If there is an odd number of spots on the die, the player who will follow the odd track moves his marker one space. If there is an even number of spots, the player on the even track moves his one space.

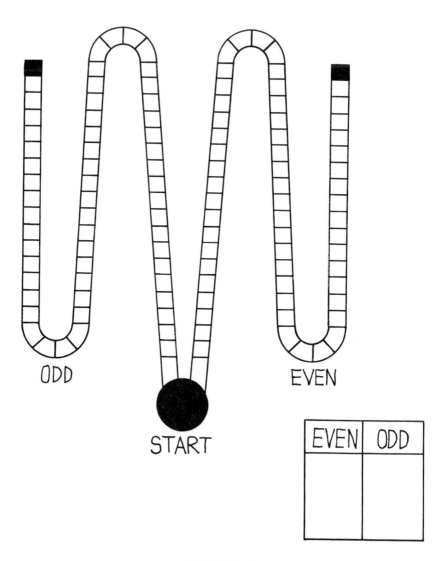

FIGURE 60

4. The players alternate rolling the die and moving their markers until one player reaches the end of his track.

5. At the end of each game the players record whether the odd or even player was winner. They should keep track of the scores for twenty to thirty games so they can see that the probabilities of winning are fifty-fifty.

Given a probability problem involving multiple events, such as rolling a die for an even number and drawing a block of a given color, the student will determine the probabilities for combination of events.

TOSS AND DRAW
(2, 4, or 6 Players)

Preparation

Use one die and a bag containing a red block and a blue block. Duplicate tally sheets such as Figure 61 for recording each team's win.

EVEN~RED	ODD~BLUE	NO WIN

FIGURE 61

Directions

1. The player(s) on one team uses the even numbers on the die and the red block as his winning combination; the other team uses the odd numbers and the blue block as his.

2. The players roll the die to determine which team goes first; the high roll plays first.

3. A player on the first team rolls the die, then draws a block from the bag. If the die and block form the right combination, the team scores one point. Otherwise, a point is put in the "no win" column of the tally sheet.

4. The game continues with the teams alternating plays until each one has rolled the die and drawn a cube twenty times.

5. The winning team is the one which scores the most points. Players should keep track of the scores for twenty to thirty games so they can determine the probabilities for a given combination occurring.

Commercial games that reinforce understanding of probability:

Shotzee

(Creative Publications)

GEOMETRY

Given models or pictures of common one-, two-, and three-dimensional geometric figures, the student will identify and name each one.

BIG-G GEOMETRY MATCH
(2–4 Players)

Preparation

Prepare two sets of playing cards on three-by-five-inch cards. One set contains pictures of geometric figures; the other contains the figures' names. Make cards for these figures: triangular prism, sphere, pyramid, cube, cone, circle, right triangle, isoceles triangle, pentagon, hexagon, septagon, octagon, decagon, parallelogram, obtuse angle, acute angle, right angle, open curve, ray, and line segment. (See Figure 62.)

Directions

1. The dealer shuffles and deals all the cards.
2. Each player stacks his cards face down in front of him.
3. At a signal from a player selected as leader, each player turns up his top card. If the picture and name of the same figure make a

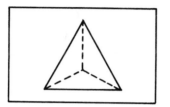 

FIGURE 62

match on two of the cards, the first player to say "Big-G" gets all the turned-up cards.

4. Play continues with players simultaneously turning up cards and looking for matching pairs. After all the cards have been played there will usually be some that are unclaimed because there have been no matches. The dealer shuffles these cards and redistributes them so players can try for additional matches.
5. A game is over when all the cards have been claimed or no matches can be made with those that remain.
6. The winner is the player who collects the most cards.

GEOMETRY MYSTERY BOX
(2–12 Players)

Preparation

Cut an arm-sized hole in each of the opposite ends of a large corrugated box. Cut out the back of the box. Prepare geometric shapes—two dimensional squares, rectangles, and three-dimensional prisms, pyramids, spheres to put inside the box. Cover the box with decorated contact paper or let children decorate it in gay colors. (See Figure 63.) Tokens are needed.

Directions

1. Place a shape inside the box.
2. The first player puts his hands through the holes and feels the shape. He earns a token if he describes the shape correctly. "This one has four square corners, all sides are the same length. It's a square."

FIGURE 63

3. If he is incorrect another player feels the shape and describes it. A correct answer earns a token.
4. After the shape has been successfully described, another shape is placed inside the box.
5. The winner is the player with the most tokens at the end of a game.

GENGO
(2–6 Players)

Preparation

Prepare six nine-by-nine-inch playing boards containing nine shapes on railroad board like the playing board in Figure 64. Arrange the shapes in a different order on each one. Cut twenty three-by-three-inch cards for pictures of the shapes. Make five cards for each shape. Cut fifty one-inch squares of railroad board for markers.

Directions

1. Each player has a playing board and eight to ten markers.
2. One child is chosen to be leader. He holds the twenty shape cards

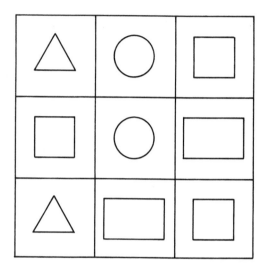

FIGURE 64

and shows them one at a time to the players. Each player covers one shape at a time on his board with the markers as the shape cards are shown.

3. The first player to cover three shapes across, down, or along a diagonal is winner.

Variations: 1. Say the name of a shape instead of showing a picture of it.
   2. Show the name of a shape instead of its picture.
   3. Have shape names on the playing boards. Show pictures or say the names.

POLYGON DRAW
(2–4 Players)

Preparation

Cut figures of triangles, quadrilaterals (squares, rectangles, and others), pentagons, and hexagons from railroad board. These figures should be both regular, i.e., congruent angles and segments, and not

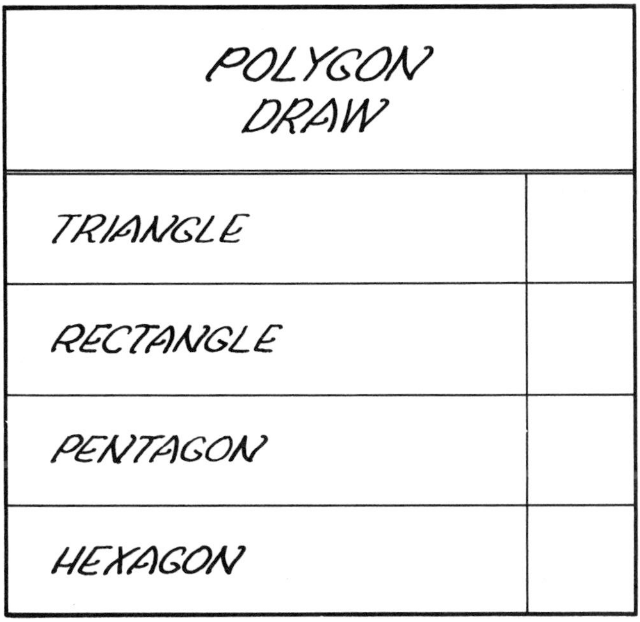

POLYGON DRAW	
TRIANGLE	
RECTANGLE	
PENTAGON	
HEXAGON	

FIGURE 65

regular. Prepare a playing board for each player like the one in Figure 65. Make a tetrahedron and mark its faces 3, 4, 5, and 6. (Directions for making a tetrahedron are on page 151 of the Appendix.)

Directions

1. Each player has a playing board. Spread the figures in the playing area within reach of each player.
2. The first player rolls the tetrahedron. He chooses a figure that has the number of sides shown on the tetrahedron and puts it on his playing board.
3. The next player takes his turn and puts his figure on his board.
4. Play continues until all figures have been drawn. When figures with a given number of sides have all been drawn, a player passes without drawing if he throws that number.
5. The winner is the player with the most figures.

GEOMETRY CONCENTRATION
(2 Players)

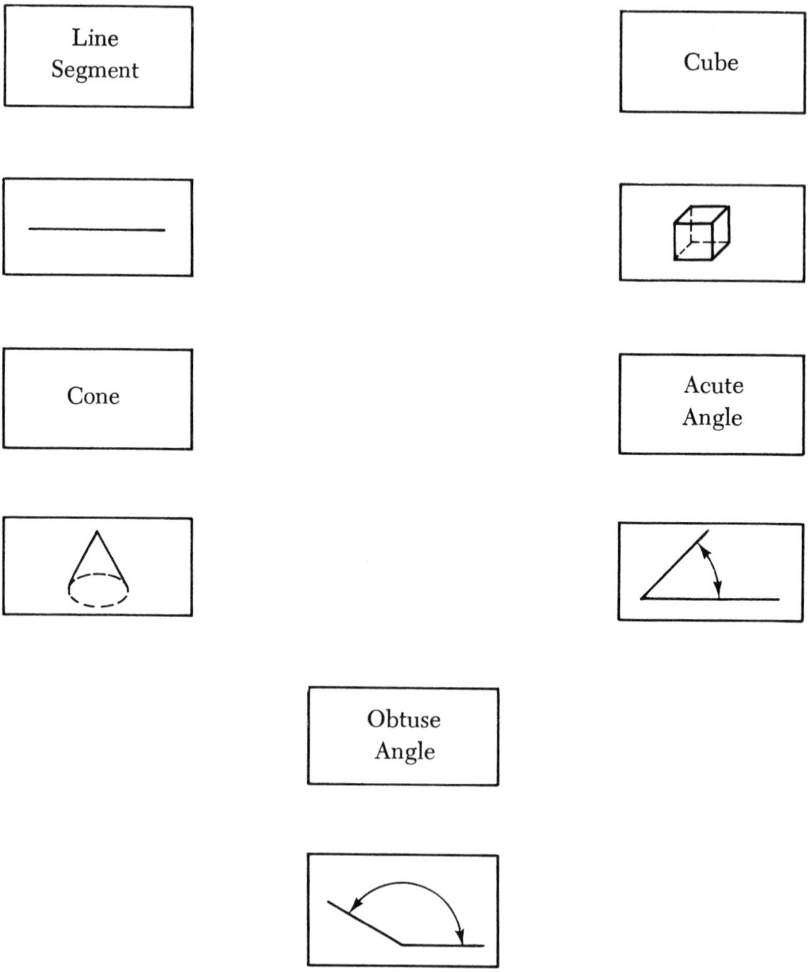

FIGURE 66

Preparation

Cut twenty three-by-four-inch cards from railroad board. Mark ten of them with pictures of geometric figures. Write each figure's name on one of the other cards. (See Figure 66.) Put a mark on the back of each card to show the bottom.

Directions

1. Put the cards face down in a four-by-five array.

2. The first player turns over two cards. If the two cards match, he keeps them and turns over another pair. If the cards do not match, they are returned to their face-down positions on the table.

3. The other player turns over two cards. If he makes a match, he keeps them and turns over another pair. If not, he returns them to the table.

4. Play continues until the twenty cards have been correctly matched.

5. The player who has the most pairs of matching cards is winner.

Variation: Use simpler shapes and fewer pairs to make an easier game.

GEOMETRY CHECKERS
(2 Players)

Preparation

Use a commercial checkerboard or make one of your own. Mark small gummed labels as shown in Figure 67 and put them on the red squares

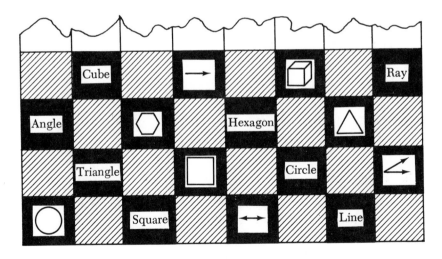

FIGURE 67

of each half, making sure to put them so the words face the player at each side of the board.

Directions

1. The rules for the game of checkers are used.
2. Before a player can move a checker he must name the shape or say the word in the square on which it will land. If he makes an error he loses his turn.

GEOMETRY LOTTO
(6 Players)

Preparation

Cut six four-by-six-inch playing boards from railroad board. Draw six squares in each one. Number the squares and draw geometric figures in them. (Figure 68 shows how to number the boxes and place the

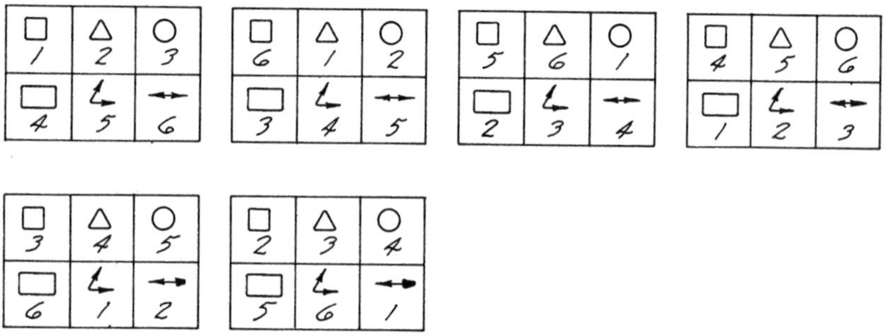

FIGURE 68

figures.) Cut thirty-six two-by-two-inch cards. Mark a card to match each of the squares on the playing boards.

Directions

1. Each player has a playing board. Mix the cards and put them face down where players can reach them easily.
2. The first player draws a shape. If it matches one of the boxes on his playing board, he names the figure and puts it on his board. If

he has no match, he looks at the other players' boards to find the
square it matches and puts it on that board.

3. Play continues with each player taking his turns in order.

4. The player whose board is covered first is winner.

GEOMETRY DOMINOES
(2–5 Players)

Preparation

Cut thirty-five two-by-four-inch dominoes from railroad board. Mark
them like the ones in Figure 69.

Directions

1. The dominoes are mixed and put face down. Each player draws
   seven.

2. One player who has been designated leader plays a double, if he
   has one. If he has none, the first player to his left who has one
   plays.

3. The rules of play for regular dominoes are used. Players can join
   figures to figures, figures to words, or words to words.

4. Each time a player puts down a piece he must name the figure or
   say the word he joins. If he is not correct he does not get to play
   the piece.

5. The winner is the player who gets rid of his dominoes first.

Variations: 1. Make a set half the size of the one shown here, showing
   only figures or words.
   2. Enlarge the set by adding more figures and words.

Given a representation of the number plane, the student
will locate ordered pairs of numbers on it.

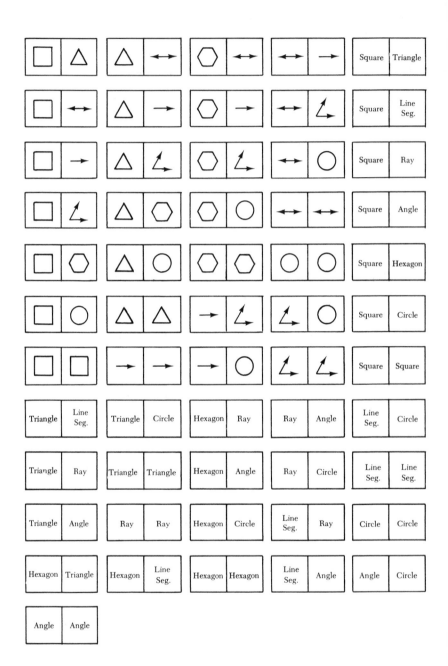

FIGURE 69

OCTACORD
(2-4 Players)

Preparation

Making a playing board like Figure 70 on a twenty-two-by-twenty-eight-inch piece of railroad board. Make the double-headed arrow at the bottom red and the one on the left side green. Make two octahedrons—one red and the other green. Number one of each of six faces

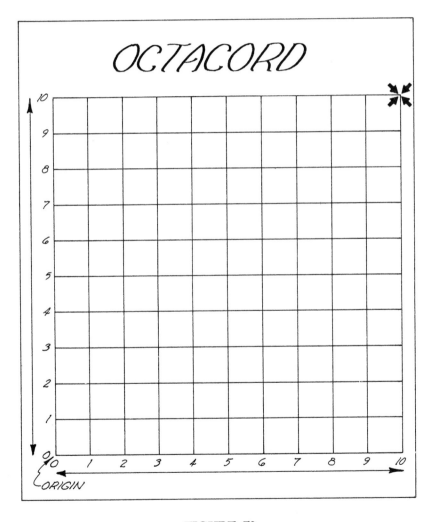

FIGURE 70

of each octahedron with a 0, 1, 2, 3, 4, or 5. Write "OCTACORD" on the other two faces. Cut twenty two-by-three-inch cards from railroad board. Write "OCTACORD" on each one. Write one of these instructions on the other side of each card:

> Take an extra turn. (Mark 3 with this)
> Lose a turn. (Mark 3 with this)
> Go to 6,4.
> Go to 8,9.
> Go to 1,9.
> Go to 7,3.
> Move left 2.
> Move left 5.
> Move up 4.
> Move up 1.
> Move right 2.
> Move right 4.
> Move down 3.
> Move down 2.
> Go back to the origin.
> Go to the point in the center of the board.

Directions

1. One player shuffles the OCTACORD cards and puts them face down on the playing board.
2. Each player puts his marker near the origin.
3. The first player rolls the two octahedron. The red one determines the number of moves to the right, while the green one determines moves up the board. These rules govern moves: a. When a numeral shows on both octahedrons the move shown by the red one is made first, then the move shown by the green one is made. b. When a numeral shows on one octahedron and OCTACORD shows on the other, the move is made first, then an OCTACORD card is drawn. A player follows the card's instruction. When he is instructed to lose a turn, he skips his next turn. He follows all other instructions immediately. c. When OCTACORD shows on both octahedron, two cards are drawn. A player may follow the instruction on whichever card he prefers first, followed by the second card's instruction. d. When a move to the right takes a marker off the playing area, a player moves it back to zero on the same line and takes his remain-

ing steps from there. When a move takes the marker off the area at the top, it is moved to the bottom and the move is completed from there.

4. OCTACORD cards are returned to the bottom of the pile after they have been played.

5. Play continues with each player taking his turns in order.

6. The winner is the player who reaches the point in the upper-right-hand corner (10, 10) first. If the time available for a game runs out before a player reaches the goal, the nearest one to it is winner.

TREASURE HUNT
(2 Players)

Preparation

Make a playing board on a piece of thirteen-by-twenty-one-inch railroad board and fold it in half. Each half of the board contains a nine-inch square number plane with 0 through 9 marked along each axis. Glue a file folder along the fold at the board's middle to separate the two halves. (See Figure 71.) This folder will hide each half from the opponent's view. Pieces of inexpensive costume or children's play jewelry and a handful of small markers for each player are needed.

Directions

1. Each player arranges one bracelet to cover three points, two broaches so each one covers two points, and three rings so each one covers one point on his number plane.

2. The first player names three points where he thinks his opponent's jewelry might be located. He puts markers on the same points on his board to keep track of his guesses. If he names a point covered by a ring, both points covered by a broach, or all three covered by a bracelet, he collects the jewelry. Otherwise, his opponent tells him if any of the points that were named are under pieces of jewelry, without telling which points they were.

3. The other player names three points where his opponent's jewelry might be located. As before, he collects jewelry when his guesses are accurate and receives word about correct and incorrect guesses.

4. The game continues with the two players taking turns in order until one player collects all his opponent's jewelry.

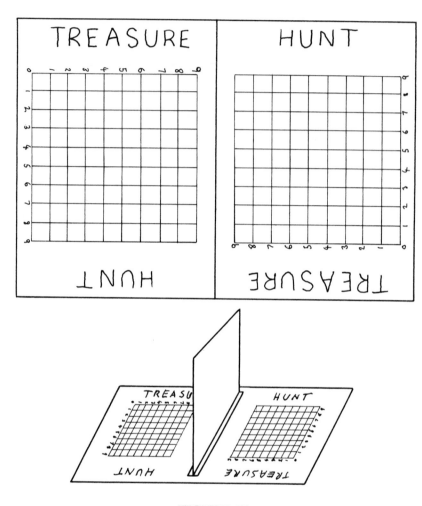

FIGURE 71

Commercial games that reinforce understanding of geometry:

Polygons
  (Creative Publications)

GeoShapes
Polyhedron—rummy
  (Scott, Foresman and Company)

Shape Chrominoes
  (Products of the Behavioral Sciences, Inc.)

PROBLEM SOLVING

Given a word problem requiring use of addition, subtraction, multiplication, or division, the student will solve
the problem.

WORD-PROBLEM SLIDE
(2-4 Players)

Preparation

Make a game board similar to the one in Figure 72 on a piece of
twenty-two-by-twenty-eight-inch railroad board. Write word problems
suitable for your children on three-by-five-inch cards. A die and
paper and pencil and a marker are needed for each player. Make a
key so players can check answers during the game.

Directions

1. One player shuffles the problem cards and puts them face down on
   the game board. Each player puts his marker in the starting square.
2. The first player rolls the die to determine how far he can move. He
   picks up the first problem card and reads it aloud. He determines

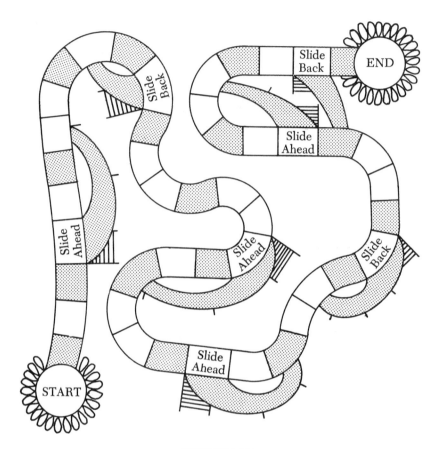

FIGURE 72

the answer, using paper and pencil if needed. If his answer is correct he moves his marker. Otherwise, he stays where he is.

3. Play continues with each player taking his turns in order.
4. The winner is the first player to reach the end.

Commercial games that reinforce problem-solving skills:

Illustrated Problem-Solving Cards
(Creative Publications)

LOGIC

Given a set of attribute materials, the student will identify and name their attributes and values.

ONE-DIFFERENCE CHAINS
(2–3 Players)

Preparation

From railroad board, make a set of attribute shapes containing three shapes, four colors, and two sizes—twenty-four pieces in all. (See Figure 73.)

Directions

1. Before a game put the shapes into manila envelopes. Use two envelopes and randomly separate the set into two subsets that each contain twelve shapes if two are playing; use three envelopes and make three subsets of eight shapes each if three are playing.
2. Each player looks at his shapes but does not show them to his opponents.
3. The first player puts one of his shapes down to start the game.

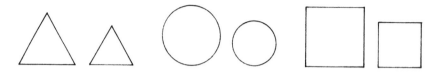

FIGURE 73

4. The next player selects a shape that differs in only one way and puts it beside the first piece. For example, if the first shape was a large yellow triangle, the next might be a small yellow triangle, a large yellow square, or a large red triangle. (There are other pieces that can be played, too.)
5. Play continues with each player putting pieces down in turn.
6. A player is blocked if he does not have a piece that differs from the last-played shape in only one way.
7. The winner is the player who gets rid of his pieces first.

Variations: 1. Enlarge the size of the set by increasing the number of shapes, colors, and/or sizes.
          2. Use two or three differences between each successive piece instead of one.

SQUARE-GRID GAME
(2–3 Players)

Preparation

Make a game board containing thirty-five four-inch squares on a twenty-two-by-twenty-eight-inch railroad board. Make a set of attribute shapes from colored railroad board. A set that has four shapes, four colors and three sizes—forty-eight pieces all together—is a good size. (See Figure 74.)

Directions

1. Before a game put the shapes into manila envelopes. Use two envelopes and randomly separate the set into two subsets that each contain twenty-four shapes if two are playing; use three envelopes

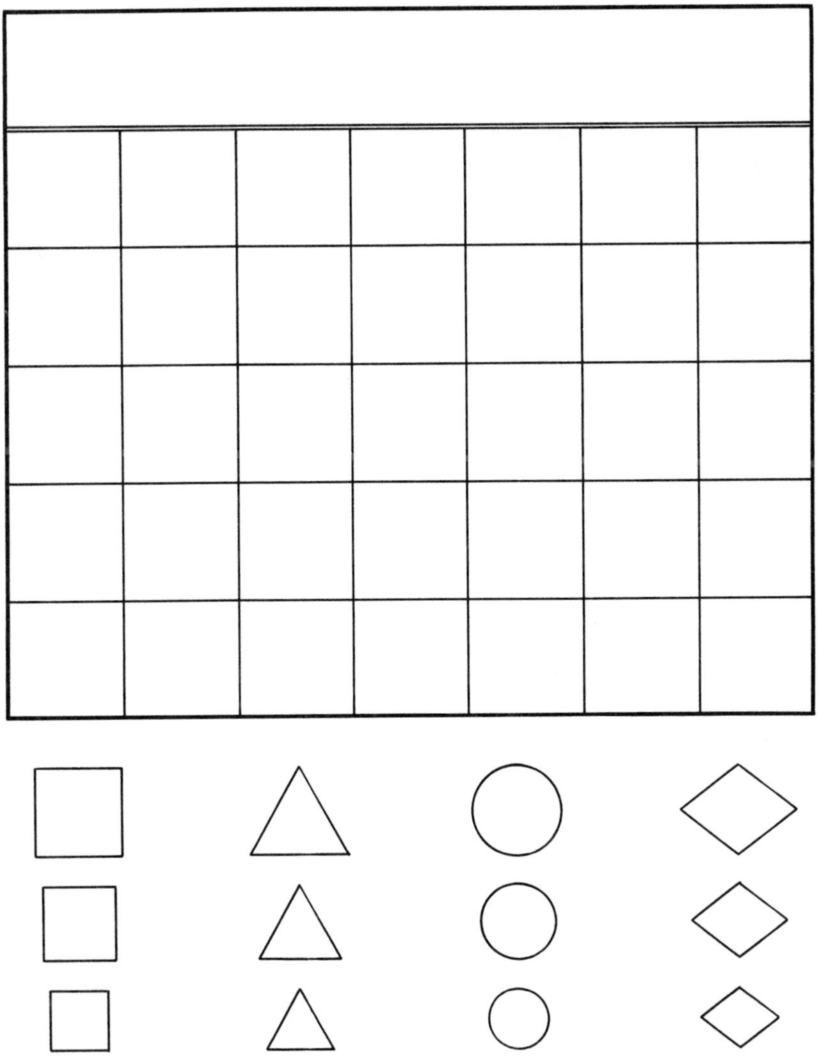

FIGURE 74

and make three subsets that each contain sixteen shapes if three are playing.

2. Each player looks at his shapes but does not show them to his opponents.

3. The first player puts one of his shapes in a square on the game board.

4. The next player selects a shape that differs from the first in one way, if he plays in the square immediately to the left or right of the first piece, or in two ways, if he plays in the square immediately above or below the first piece.

5. Play continues with each player taking turns in order putting pieces on the grid, according to the rules of one difference across and two differences up and down.

6. A player is blocked when he does not have a piece he can play.

7. The winner is the player who gets rid of his shapes first.

Variation: Change the number of differences between pieces required for making plays.

Commercial games:

Giant Attribute Blocks
Pocket Attribute Set
Giant Attribute Guide
Attribute Games and Problems
  (Creative Publications)

MISCELLANEOUS

These are games that deal with more than one mathematical concept. They are used to reinforce children's skills with the concepts they cover.

PICK
(3–5 Players)

(This game reinforces children's understanding that a number has many names.)

Preparation

Make a deck of fifty-two playing cards divided into four suits on three-by-five-inch cards. Write the words for the numbers 1 through 13 on thirteen cards. Write the numerals for the numbers on another thirteen. Put addition combinations, one for each number, on thirteen, and subtraction combinations, one for each number, on the other thirteen. (See Figure 75.)

Directions

1. The dealer shuffles the cards and deals six to each player. The rest of the cards are put face down in a draw pile.

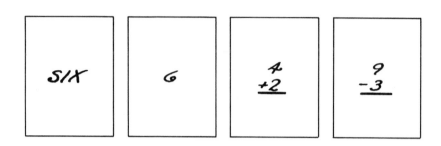

FIGURE 75

2. The player to the dealer's left has the first play. If he has four cards that match, he puts them face up in front of him. Whether or not he has four matching cards he asks the player on his left for a card which will help complete one of his sets, "Do you have any _____?" If the player has any of the cards of this set, he passes them. If he has none, he says "Pick" and the first player takes a card from the draw pile. If he makes a four-card match by either asking or drawing, he puts the set down immediately. Play passes to the next player.

3. Play continues with each player taking his turns in order until one is rid of all of his cards.

4. The winner is the player who builds the most sets.

MATHEMATICAL GOLF*
(2–4 Players)

(This game reinforces children's understanding of number relations.)

Preparation

Make duplicate copies of the score card shown in Figure 76. Each player can use his own or one card can be used for all the players. Two dice and a pencil are needed.

Directions

1. The first player rolls the dice until he gets a 1 on either cube. The number of times he rolls them to do this is his score for the hole.

---

* We thank Ed Arnsdorf for this game.

MATHEMATICAL GOLF

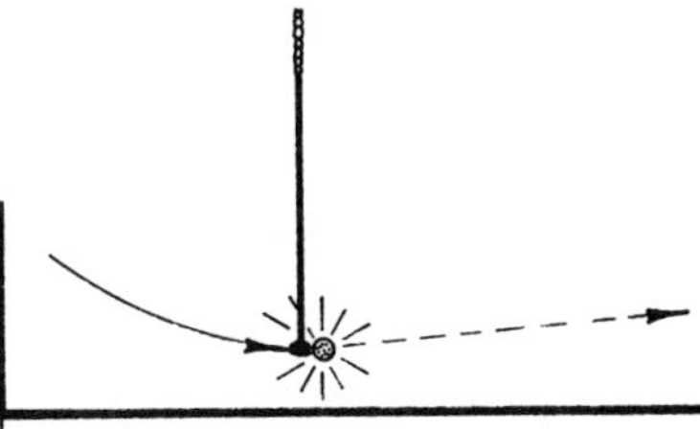

HOLE	PAR					
						PUT EACH PLAYER'S NAME IN ONE OF THE BOXES.
1	3					A ONE SHOWS ON EITHER CUBE.
2	3					SUM IS DIVISIBLE BY TWO.
3	4					SUM IS DIVISIBLE BY THREE.
4	4					SUM IS A MULTIPLE OF FOUR.
5	5					SUM IS < 5.
6	3					A SIX SHOWS ON EITHER CUBE
7	5					THE SUM = 7.
8	4					THE SUM IS A PRIME.
9	4					THE SUM $\geq$ 9.
PAR	35					

SCORES

FIGURE 76

2. Each of the players rolls until he gets a 1 and records his score.

3. Play continues with each player rolling the dice to score for the remaining holes. The number of rolls needed for each player to complete each hole is recorded on the score sheet. Each one takes his turns in order until the nine holes have been completed.

4. At the end of the game each player adds his scores.

5. The winner is the player with the low score.

Variations: 1. Change some of the requirements for scoring points at

the various holes to increase or lessen the game's difficulty.
2. Add another nine holes to give a round of eighteen holes.

PROBLEMS IN TENTHS
(*2–4 Players*)

(This game reinforces children's understanding of problems involving
decimal tenths.)

$0.2 = $ __%

Write by tenths from 6 to 7	Write by tenths from 0–1

Write 1/10 as a decimal	Write 2/10 as a decimal

At the beginning of a
trip, a car's odometer
read 456.2 miles. At

(Make difficulty to suit level)

the end it read 542.1.
What was the trip's
length?

Write 0.8 as a
common fraction

FIGURE 77

Preparation

On three-by-five-inch cards make thirty-six problem cards involving tenths written as decimal fractions. Figure 77 suggests types of problems to include. Each player will need paper and pencil so he can record his answers. Make a key so players can check answers at the end of the game.

Directions

1. The dealer shuffles the cards and deals them.
2. Each player works the problems on his cards and records his answers.
3. Each player's answers are checked and the right ones counted.
4. The winner is the player who has the most right answers.

FRACTION RUMMY
(2–5 Players)

(These games reinforce children's understanding of the common and decimal fraction and percent expressions for fractional numbers.)

Preparation

Make playing cards containing pictures that show fractional numbers represented by parts of regions, sets, and lines, and expressed as common fractions, decimal fractions, and percent forms of representation. Use three-by-five-inch cards to show these fractional numbers: 1/2, 1/3, 2/3, 1/4, 3/4, 1/5, 2/5, 3/5, 4/5, 1/6, 5/6, 1/8, 3/8, 5/8, 7/8. The four cards, which make a "book" for 1/2 are illustrated in Figure 78. Make a key showing a picture of each fraction and its numeral expressions so children can check answers during play.

Directions

1. The dealer shuffles the cards and deals seven to each player. The rest of the cards are put face down in a draw pile. The top card is turned over.
2. The player to the dealer's left has the first play. If he has three or four cards that match, he puts them face up in front of him. Whether

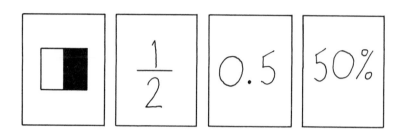

FIGURE 78

or not he has cards to lay down, he draws from the draw pile or the turned-up card. If the card he draws gives him a three-card match, he puts the cards down. Otherwise, he discards the card or puts it in his hand and discards another.

3. Play passes to the next player, who puts down any three- or four-card matches he holds. He completes his play by making his draw and discard. When a player wants a card below the top card in the discard pile he can take it only if he takes all the·cards above it, too.

4. Play continues with each player taking his turns in order until one player is rid of all of his cards.

5. The scores for a round are determined in this way: points are awarded according to each card a player has put down. For example, a player who puts down three matching cards for 1/3, scores 1/3 of a point for each, or a total of 1 point. Each player who holds cards at a round's end determines their total and subtracts it from the points he earned for the cards he played.

6. The winner is the player who has earned the most points during a given number of rounds.

TAKE A TRICK
(2–4 Players)

Preparation

Make a deck containing forty-eight cards on three-by-five-inch cards. Mark twelve of the cards so they contain pictures for fractional numbers represented by parts of regions, sets, or line segments. Mark them

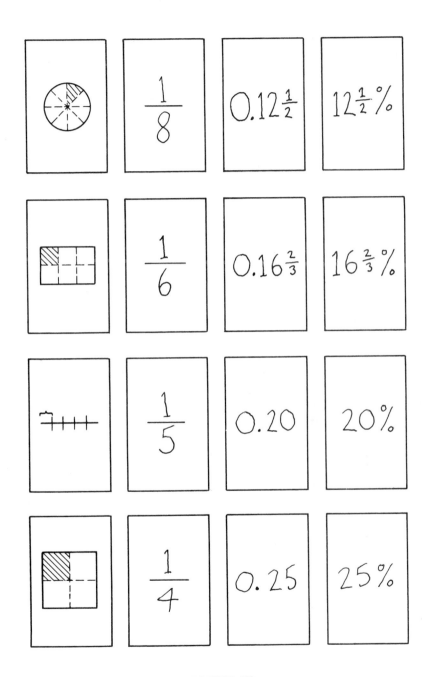

FIGURE 79

in one color of ink. Write the common fraction, decimal fraction, and percent expressions for each fractional number on the other thirty-six cards. Use three different colors to mark these cards, one color for each representation. Make a table showing the pictures and the numeral expressions for players to use as an answer key during the game. (See Figure 79.)

Directions

1. The dealer shuffles and deals all the cards.
2. The player to the dealer's left puts one of his cards face up in the center of the playing area.
3. Playing in a clockwise direction, each player puts a card of the same color on the one played. The player who plays the card representing the largest fraction takes the four cards. When a player does not have a card the same color as the one played, he can put down one of another color. He cannot take the four cards when he does this, even though his card may represent a larger fraction than any of the other three.
4. The player who takes the four cards puts down the first one for the next round.
5. Play continues until all the cards have been played.
6. At the end of play each player selects the card that represents the largest fraction in each suit from the ones he collected. His score is the sum of these cards. (If need be, a player can use paper and pencil to change the fractions to one kind and add.)
7. The winner is the player with the highest total for the round. Or, he can be the player with the highest total at the end of a given number of rounds.

APPENDIX

Pattern for Spinner

Cut each piece from ¼-inch masonite or ¼-inch clear plastic. Glue the small square shown in Figure 80 on page 148 to the center of the large one. Drill a ¼-inch hole and glue a one-inch long ¼-inch dowel in the hole. Enlarge the hole in the pointer so it turns freely.

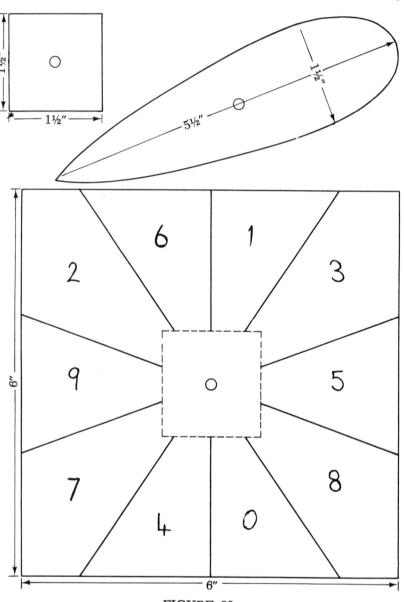

FIGURE 80

Pattern for Card Holder

Fold along the dotted lines indicated in Figure 81. Overlap the two end pieces and glue them to make the base.

Card Holder

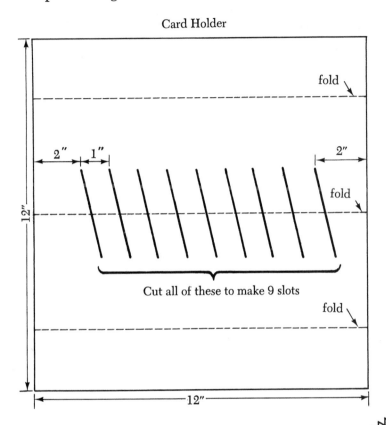

FIGURE 81

Pattern for Pocket Card Holder

Cut a six-by-nine-inch piece of railroad board. Measure up two inches and fold along the dotted line. Staple the folded part to the back to form the number of pockets needed for a game. Label as indicated by the game's illustration.

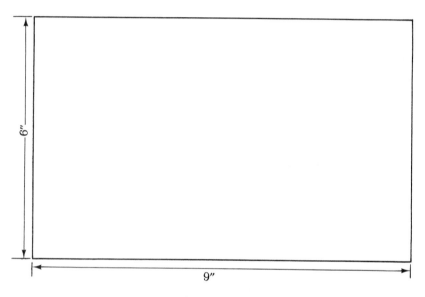

Pocket Card Holder

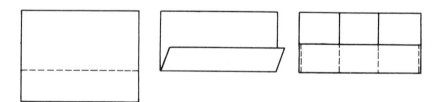

FIGURE 82

Pattern for Tetrahedron

Tetrahedron

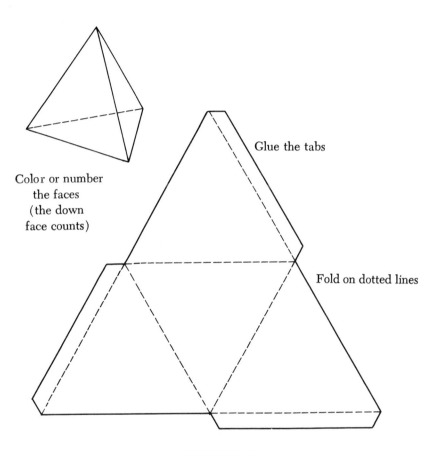

Glue the tabs

Color or number
the faces
(the down
face counts)

Fold on dotted lines

FIGURE 83

Pattern for Cube

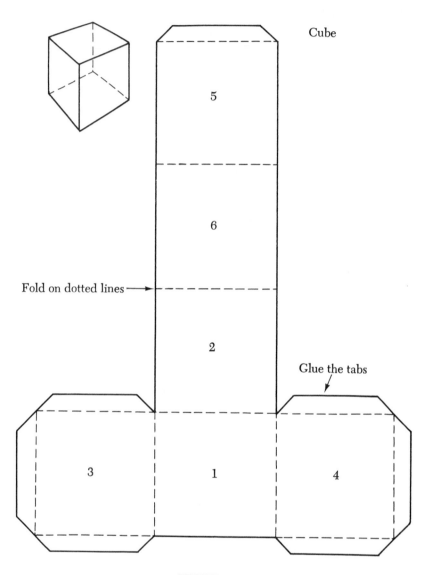

Cube

5

6

Fold on dotted lines →

2

Glue the tabs

3   1   4

FIGURE 84

Pattern for Octahedron

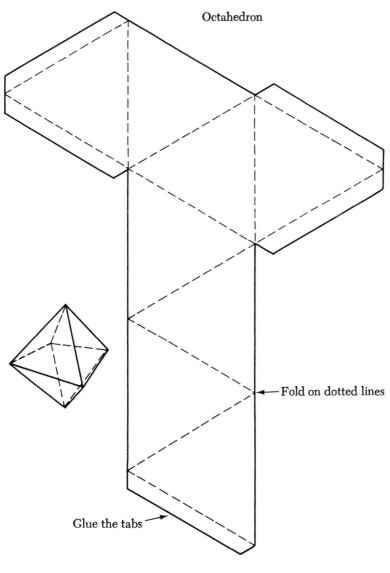

Octahedron

Fold on dotted lines

Glue the tabs

FIGURE 85

Pattern for Dodecahedron

Dodecahedron

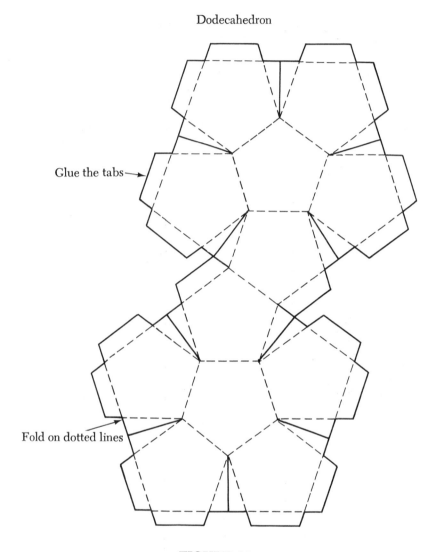

FIGURE 86

Distributors of Mathematical Games

A. R. Davis and Co.
P. O. Box 24424
San Jose, Ca. 95154

Creative Publications
P. O. Box 10328
Palo Alto, Ca. 94303

Cuisenaire Company of America
12 Church Street
New Rochelle, N.Y. 10805

Gamco Industries, Inc.
Box 1911 B
Big Springs, Texas 79720

IMOUT Arithmetic Drill Games
706 Williamson Building
Cleveland, Ohio 44114

Marie's Educational Materials
P. O. Box 694
Sunnyvale, Ca. 94086

Products of the Behavioral Sciences, Inc.
1140 Dell Ave.
Campbell, Ca. 95008

Scott, Foresman and Co.
1900 East Lake Ave.
Glenview, Ill. 60025